Patience

and

Prayer

By Gregory Heary

Patience and Prayer are two primary means of receiving the help we seek, for the Creator has commanded us to observe them and promised them to be the recipe for receiving help from him. Both are obligatory to observe and forbidden to neglect. Though they are not of equal importance having one without the other in your life will cause extremism and imbalance in the individual/society. As both are so important to our belief and lifestyle I have decided to compose this collection of Quranic ayat and hadith on patience and the virtues/rewards of prayer to serve as a reminder and tool so that we can increase the quality and quantity of our patience and prayers. Thereby the believing reader who reflects and remembers may potentially qualify for the divinely promised help that is better than what we ask and hope for.

Consider the birds and how they wake up every morning hungry not knowing where they will find food for the day. They don't despair, they remember Allah patiently trusting that they will be provided for and go out to search for their daily bounty. Despite all the odds being against them, with intense competition from their own species as well as others and the threat of predators, they still find food to eat each and every bird, each and every day. Most birds never storing anything for the next day and always being grateful to their maker and the maker of their food. Then the environment changes and is no longer a good place for them to be in. Despite having been born, raised and living in that location their entire lives, they migrate somewhere else taking nothing with them but themselves. Always putting complete trust in Allah knowing he will provide for them in their new location wherever it may be, as promised. Then it turns out that someone builds a birdhouse for the bird to use, without the bird ever asking them to. Allah used humans to provide shelter for the birds without the birds ever expecting it. Likewise Allah will provide shelter for us from places unexpected as long as we are like the birds and ask Allah for shelter then we will have it, if Allah wills. On the other hand if we ignore Allah and ask humans to provide for us then it would be similar to the bird asking the human to build a birdhouse, the human might help or they might be irritated by the bird and drive it away. The birds worship the Creator, they'll accept crumbs given to them by humans, even disbelieving humans, but they know that Allah is the provider and that the humans are just the temporary tool of sustenance that Allah chose to send food their way at that moment. If the human giving crumbs to the bird tries to harm it or inhibit it from living the way Allah wants it to the bird flies away from their birdhouse and doesn't return, no matter how many crumbs the oppressive human offers, the bird chooses its religion and its rights over the tasty crumbs. Unfortunately many humans think if they don't get crumbs from other humans then they will not get any crumbs whatsoever and they compromise their religion for the meager crumbs. Whereas if they were like the birds and fled a crumb giver who was wrong, they would have found the new source of sustenance given by the Creator would have been more plentiful and nutritious, with increased benefit even if it were less in quantity. Even the food birds eat, worms, migrate when their environment hampers their religion. Such as when it's raining out, the worms move elsewhere to avoid drowning. Yet when we are drowning in a sinful environment we never even consider moving someplace else. Then if we do, we make the mistake some worms make by thinking they can safely stay out in the sun and never go back to their previous place or elsewhere despite the conditions having changed, thus some worms get scorched because they don't emigrate every time they should. I mention this because in regards to Muslims praying 5 times a day, some will say, "*If you got a job you can't just stop working and pray, you're getting paid to work.*" To that I say, "*Well they give coffee breaks at work, they give lunch breaks at work, they give smoking breaks at work, they give breaks to poop and they give breaks to pee. That's 5 types of breaks right there. So if you can get a break to pee you can get a break to pray!*" Personally I'd willingly give up a lunch break and all the rest in exchange for a prayer break, or I'd just work extra time for free in order to pray on time during working hours. I'd work on sundays, saturdays, all the unislamic holidays, days, nights, overtime, but prayer time is prayer time and there's no compromises when it comes to prayer. Most jobs give employees entire days off, so to not give employees a few minutes during work to pray is a crime. Its actually illegal in most countries too to not let Muslims take prayer breaks at work, in some countries its even illegal to not let Muslim employees pray all their prayers in the masjid. Plus it's not good business either. God is not going to bless a business that prohibits humans from taking a break from working to worship him at the time he commands them to do so. Also an employee that can't perform their prayers will suffer in their work performance. If breaks can be given at work in order to perform bodily functions, for nutrition, relaxation or developing co-worker relationships, then surely time must be given for the spiritual nutrition, relaxation and development of the relationship with God that's strengthened through prayer. A company that doesn't let it's workers pray isn't a profitable company worth working for. No employer-employee contracts can take precedent over the contract one makes with God. When one agrees to worship Allah, the shahada is their contract with God. Thus employers must realize Muslims do not have the legal right to offer 24/7 service because their Creator has created them to pray at certain times of the day for a few minutes and some of those prayers(like Friday prayer and Eid prayers) have specific locations they are prayed in. People like to quip that prayer is the best wireless connection but they forget that different locations have different levels of reception. For example a church and toilet are not places that are fit to pray in whereas masjids have stronger reception and angels are there too and those angels ask forgiveness for those who are inside. So just because a Muslim may be able to pray in many different places, those places are not equal and some are better than others and some are forbidden to pray in, such as a toilet, graveyard or a church. Anyways a good boss wouldn't mind a Muslim employee praying in the masjid and returning to work, because they would know how allowing Muslim men to go pray in the masjid instead of the office would make them even better workers and bring blessings to the company. Personally I was unemployed for 11 years, and actually refused to take a job that didn't allow me to pray at work, then I almost reported that company to the government for such illegal discrimination but before I could Allah blessed me with a better job, as promised. Also keep in mind I'm not saying that Muslims should get paid by their employer for praying. I actually think they shouldn't get paid while praying but should stop the work clock while praying, eating, drinking, peeing and pooping. No employees should be paid for pooping, unless they are a professional pooper. Yet if the wages aren't paid based on time spent working, which I think employees should be paid based on the work that gets done instead of the time it takes them to do the work, then there shouldn't even be an issue with Muslims praying 5 times a day as long as they get all their work done on schedule. Which if the

Muslim man is punctual in praying on-time 5 times a day, he's going to be getting his work done on schedule too. Whereas Muslim women shouldn't even be working outside the home, because they should get taken care of by their husband or family and Islam says it's more rewarding for women to pray at home, but for men it's more rewarding to pray in the masjid. Also to put in perspective just how important prayer in the masjid is for a Muslim man there is the example of the Muslims during the time of Muhammad pbuh. Like married men and women do, sometimes they had sexual intercourse. In Islam when you do that you have to wash afterwards before you can pray. Well prayer was so important to Muslims and Muslim men that sometimes the call to prayer would be heard while Muslim men were having intercourse with their wives. Do you know what they did? They stopped having intercourse and came to pray and asked Muhammad pbuh whether they should do wudu or ghusl because they were having intercourse but they didn't finish so they didn't know if they should do the regular ablutions or the full-body ablutions required after one ejaculates. At first Muhammad pbuh informed them that when such a thing happens (the time for prayer comes when in the midst of intercourse) they should make the regular ablution (wudu) but also wash their penis as long as they hadn't ejaculated. Later on Muslims became more used to the timings of the prayers so that they tended not be having intercourse when it was time to pray and thus this ruling of just doing wudu in such a situation was abrogated and Muslims were instructed to do a full-body ablution (ghusl) after intercourse even if they haven't ejaculated. Yet the main lesson to draw from this is that Muslim spouses loved prayer so much and gave it so much importance in their life that they would actually stop having intercourse in order to pray in the masjid on time. This is because prayer on time in the masjid is so important and it's fun. The wretched Non-Muslims don't understand this, but praying correctly the Islamic way is more fun than having sex. How many men would do such a thing today and stop in the midst of intercourse with their wife in order to come to pray at the masjid on time? How many newlyweds would do that? Thus if Muslims interrupted their sexual relations in order to pray on time and at the masjid, do you think a true practicing Muslim is going to think "work" is too important for them to interrupt in order to pray on time and/or in the masjid? So there actually is no issue at all with work and prayer for Muslims, the issue is people wrongly consider work to be more important than worship so they schedule their worship around their work when it's supposed to be the other way around. For a Muslim man if they pray in the masjid they get the reward for that prayer multiplied by 27 times than if they did their obligatory prayer outside the masjid, they still have to do 5 everyday but they would get 27 times the reward because they do it in the masjid. That's the reason why I started going to the American masjids, despite my initial apprehension. My concerns over surveillance and undercover agents were unfounded and it was simply the government trying to frighten Muslims away from the masjid so less people pray in it. They fear the power of Muslim prayers in the masjid. The ultimate goal of unislamic governments is to prevent Muslims from going to pray 5 times a day in the masjid and claiming to put undercover agents in them helps them stop Muslims from praying there and distract/disunite ignorant Muslims. So they say it and sometimes do it just to intimidate Muslims and decrease masjid attendance. Regardless every masjid already comes with special agents anyways surveilling the Muslims recording all they do, they are called angels. All people have always been under surveillance with special agents observing their speech and deeds reporting it to one who can severely punish them if they say or do something islamically wrong. Thus one must never fear going to pray in the masjid, it is Satan that instills such fears. The pagans in Mecca tried to scare the early Muslims away from the masjid too, but the success was in being patient with the abuse, surveillance and harassment on the road to paradise. Masjids are the houses of Allah for his slaves to get the best prayer reception in and protection from Satan and enjoy the company of angels and believers alike. Even if some evil kafir goons were present to spy therein, which from my experience they aren't, that is their business and Muslims are going to say and do the same stuff regardless of who is watching or listening because our thoughts, speech and deeds are determined only by our concern for the Creator who is watching and listening. Even during the life of Muhammad pbuh there were many undercover non-Muslims in the masjid in Medinah to spy on the Muslims, yet they all came to pray; despite knowing 100% there were spies there because the Quran told them there were. When one truly knows Allah is watching them they don't care about what anything else may think or do to them in anticipation or due to a reaction. Rather than fear the enemies of Islam the Muslims should be more afraid and embarrassed of what Allah thinks and will do to them for not praying in the masjids rather than what disbelievers will think and do if they prayed on time in masjids, because Allah does know and is much more important. The excuse that praying in a masjid may decrease one's wealth is false because it is Allah who sends the wealth and personally I and all the others who attend masjids can testify that wealth increases if one attends masjids regularly with sincerity, despite what worldly projections may predict. Also the excuse of "time" is invalid because I have tried life both ways and I've found that I have more time to do stuff when I pray in the masjid than when I don't, so a person's gift of time is blessed when it is invested in the masjid. It is a shame to see birds have more faith and trust in Allah than humans, especially considering humans are given so much more to be grateful for than birds. You and I can probably plan what we will eat tomorrow and perhaps for the rest of the week, we may even have enough food to last for months. At the least we could likely afford to survive for many days without receiving any further sustenance. We likely have clothes to wear, technology, food aplenty and shelter to protect us from the weather. We've eaten more food than we could ever store or count. How ungrateful are we for the bounties Allah has bestowed? The foolish say *"God helps him who helps himself"*, and the extremely foolish think the bible says that but it's both unbiblical and false. That quote comes from the greek philosopher Aesop, most famous for his fables. God helps every creature because we wouldn't even exist had God not helped us, but God helps the grateful believers more in proportion to their belief and gratitude. God will help everyone but in different ways, for example God helped both Moses pbuh and Pharaoh as well as both David pbuh and Goliath. However God helped all of them in very different ways because they were different people. The thing is that God does not help everyone equally though he helps all. To get more blessings from God you have to believe and obey God more than other people, if you want God to treat you the best then you have to be the best friend of God. God helps both friends and enemies, which will you be? Regardless God doesn't help anyone for free, and since God always helps everyone that means everyone always owes

God. Fortunately God will forgive the debts his friends owe, and pays them with paradise. God's enemies though must pay the unpayable price, which since it can't ever be repaid then they will never stop paying the price for being a disobedient ungrateful enemy of God whose sins are not forgiven. Whether you like it or not you already owe God. So will you wisely choose to be God's friend or his enemy? Performing the prophetic prayer is 1 way to pay God today. People mistakenly think practicing a religion and living the way God wants requires extreme sacrifices, but they are wrong. To enter paradise you just have to accept and fulfill the terms on the bargain price that God is selling paradise for. The prophets came to tell us about a bargain offer that God desires us to accept, namely to sell him our souls and life in exchange for paradise. Which truly is a great bargain considering God gave us our soul and life to begin with. God has offered us a great deal, given us all we need to make this transaction and God wants to help us succeed in this bargain by helping us every step of the way until our transaction is complete when the angel of death takes us to meet our Lord. As explained before, praying to God in the way his prophet's taught us is a key pillar of this bargain transaction between the Creator, Judge and Sustainer. Without the patient prayer in the prophetic matter the bargain deal falls through and the transaction of submission in exchange for admission/salvation will not take place. Praying prophetically is to profit now and later. God is as his servant hopes, but many misunderstand this assuming they are a true servant of God and that their hopes are realistic or that they even fulfilled the criteria to have hopes. For example if you barely do any work for your human employer and tell them you hope for a promotion to the highest position imaginable they will explain that your hopes are unrealistic because your actions don't match your ambitions. So the key to having hope is to do actions. If you want the best spot in paradise or even a position that is not in hell then your actions should justify your hopes. Everyone hopes to pass the tests they take, including the test of life but not everyone does because their actions don't coincide with their dreams. You can get more than what you hope for from God, but you need to do more than just hope. The way to have hope is by holding onto the rope of prophetic guidance that God has sent no matter how hard it is to climb that rope for the rest of your life in every condition without deviation all the way to the top level in paradise. The servant of God can justifiably hope for the best by being and doing their best. A hopeful servant is hopeful of reward not because of merely hoping and being a servant of a generous master, but because they do some pretty good serving; for life. And just as servants are given a list of daily duties, one of the greatest duties of a servant of God is their daily prayer which is incomplete without patience.

Some creatures are not only ungrateful but don't want others to be grateful and even forbid people from praying to God and expressing gratitude. For instance non-Muslims will tell me "*I can't pray 24 hours a day like you do.*" and it leaves me speechless because I do not pray 24 hours a day. Do you think I'd be able to write this book if I was praying 24 hours a day? To write a book of this length would be impossible if I "*just prayed all day*". Yet if I didn't pray 5 times every day I'd never be able to have written this book. Because the one who has time without prayers has no blessings in their time, regardless of the quantity it is of worthless quality. Many non-Muslims get confused if you tell them God created people so they can worship him they take it to mean you are saying they should live in a monastery and do nothing but eat/fast, sleep and pray. Worship is not just prayer, but the Islamic prayers themselves aren't long at all. Most non-Muslims get shocked by "5 prayers a day" and arrogantly say they just don't have the time because they got a job or responsibilities, as if everyone of the 2 billion+ Muslims on the planet don't. Each Islamic prayer takes about 5-10 minutes, so 5 prayers of about 5 minutes every day amounts to about 25 minutes of obligatory prayers a day. Doesn't every person have 25 minutes to pray to God everyday? Is 25 minutes equal to 24 hours? NO! The worse part about people complaining that Islam requires 5 prayers a day is that those who tell me they can't do it and don't have time, actually have an abundance of time to do it. They just don't want to so they say they can't. For example a typical short tv show lasts 30 minutes. This means if you watch on average 1 tv show a day then you have more than enough time to pray 5 times a day. If they can watch a sports game once a week then they definitely have time to pray much more than 5 times a day. Yet those who insist they can't, not only tend to watch tv on a daily basis but watch movies, play video games, listen to music, use their computer to surf the internet and so many other things for hours and hours every day. So the real reason they claim they don't have the time is because they are stuck in front of their TV idol praying to that and don't want to quit or reduce the amount of their daily devotions to entertainment. It's not that they don't have time to pray, they just want to use their time doing other things instead, usually sinful things. Then they'll dare to say Muslims are lazy and just pray to get out of doing work or something. Ironically this is the same thing a bible says Pharaoh told Moses pbuh and Muslims in Exodus 5:1-17 according to the NIV bible,

*"Afterward Moses and Aaron went to Pharaoh and said, "This is what the Lord, the God of Israel, says: 'Let my people go, so that they may hold a festival to me in the wilderness.'"² Pharaoh said, "Who is the Lord, that I should obey him and let Israel go? I do not know the Lord and I will not let Israel go." ³ Then they said, "The God of the Hebrews has met with us. Now let us take a three-day journey into the wilderness to offer sacrifices to the Lord our God, or he may strike us with plagues or with the sword."⁴ **But the king of Egypt said, "Moses and Aaron, why are you taking the people away from their labor? Get back to your work!"** ⁵ **Then Pharaoh said,** "Look, the people of the land are now numerous, and **you are stopping them from***

<u>working."</u> [6] That same day Pharaoh gave this order to the slave drivers and overseers in charge of the people: [7] "You are no longer to supply the people with straw for making bricks; let them go and gather their own straw. [8] But require them to make the same number of bricks as before; don't reduce the quota. **<u>They are lazy; that is why they are crying out, 'Let us go and sacrifice to our God.' [9] Make the work harder for the people so that they keep working and pay no attention to lies."</u>** [10] Then the slave drivers and the overseers went out and said to the people, "This is what Pharaoh says: 'I will not give you any more straw. [11] Go and get your own straw wherever you can find it, but your work will not be reduced at all.'" [12] So the people scattered all over Egypt to gather stubble to use for straw. [13] The slave drivers kept pressing them, saying, "Complete the work required of you for each day, just as when you had straw." [14] And Pharaoh's slave drivers beat the Israelite overseers they had appointed, demanding, "Why haven't you met your quota of bricks yesterday or today, as before?"[15] Then the Israelite overseers went and appealed to Pharaoh: "Why have you treated your servants this way? [16] Your servants are given no straw, yet we are told, 'Make bricks!' Your servants are being beaten, but the fault is with your own people."[17] **<u>Pharaoh said, "Lazy, that's what you are — lazy! That is why you keep saying, 'Let us go and sacrifice to the Lord.' "</u>**

Does this scenario sound familiar? It's the same type of thing many people tell believers today who desire nothing other than to pray and obey their prophet's instructions to worship their Creator at the times or places they are told to do so. Modern Pharaohs will say, "*If you got all that time to pray then that means you ain't working hard enough. If you worked hard like me you wouldn't have the time or energy to pray.*" They'll say you're lazy, crazy and that God doesn't want you to pray the way, times or places the prophets told you to. Which again is exactly what a bible says that the tyrannical Pharaoh said, "***They are lazy; that is why*** *they are crying out, 'Let us go and sacrifice to our God.' 9 Make the work harder for the people so that they keep working and **pay no attention to lies**.*" Yet modern Pharaohs will go even further and they'll say God wants you to work and they'll say your religious books say so too, thus if you aren't working you must not be following your religion. At least Pharaoh was decent enough not to tell Moses pbuh that God didn't want Moses pbuh to pray at X time in Y location. The tyrants today will even say God hates you for praying because work is so important and that praying to God instead of working is making God upset with you. These silly people don't know the first thing about religion. One is commanded to work only to prevent themselves from begging, that's all. If you aren't begging then you don't truly "need" to be working. Although even if one were to be broke and begging the prayer still takes priority over working. Because when begging, God is the first one you beg and you do so in your prayer. This is because work doesn't create wealth. Just as how flicking a light switch doesn't by itself create light, the proper connections must exist and everything in the circuit must be in correct alignment for flicking the light switch to produce light. There are steps to follow as well as a specific order to follow, in order to achieve success. Sincerity and Knowledge are vital. Doing the work of flipping the switch is the last step, not the first step or the only, nor is it the most important. If you flip the switch and decide to make the proper connections later, you will get electrocuted. Likewise if prayer is not a part of your life, you will get hurt in a broken circuit that will be guaranteed to result in spiritual poverty, moral bankruptcy and a hardened heart of darkness. If you just do work as your first and only step towards getting wealth, you will get hurt in a major way. To go along with these deadly afflictions gained for the sake of material wealth, one still won't get the wealth unless God is generous to them, but even if God is there will be no blessings in it and it will only lead to their destruction because they are working for other than God. Thus by them working instead of praying, God will actually be upset with them and hate them for working. Thereby working will become a huge sin for them and their wealth will be sinful. This is because when God invites them to pray they ignore and reject God's calls falsely claiming they are busy working or doing something else. They are telling God there are more important things to do than doing what he tells them to do. Yet God knows our life and defines what is "important". God won't command us to pray at certain times if we really can't. If God commanded prayer for us then we can do it, the only question is whether we will do it, or if we let some Pharaoh deter us, or if we become our own Pharaoh and choose to deter ourselves because Satan tells us we can't even though we can and must. Every single person I have ever met can pray the Islamic prayers 5 times a day, and I've examined their daily schedules when they claim they can't or don't have time and they all can and do have time. Thus those thinking they can't, should think again because I swear to God they can if they want to do so. If anyone says they can't then just ask them directly *"Do you want to?"* If so then they will do it no matter what. For instance Muslim men prostrate during their prayers but there are exceptions if one is unable to prostrate then they could sit in a chair or something during that part of the prayer, if they really can't do it. However some people I know say they can't become Muslim because they can't prostrate in prayer due to their age or leg problems. Whereas if they really can't prostrate then they don't have to because Allah gives such people an exemption due to inability, so if they have a problem that prevents them praying 100% the prophetic way then it's no problem, they don't have to do every gesture if they physically can't; if you can't prostrate you can still be Muslim and have all your prayers count. Yet typically such people simply don't want to be Muslim or pray so they make lame excuses like that thinking they can fool God or me into believing them. I'm not fooled by such excuses so God definitely isn't either. It all comes down to *"Do you want to worship God as best as possible the way God wants you to? It's not about if you can it's whether you want to or not. Do you want to?"* If so then people find a way because they ask God to help them and help is provided, as is promised.

For example once I prayed next to a guy who only had 1 leg, his other leg was missing from the knee down. So since he couldn't stand on one leg he was sitting in a chair during the standing part of the prayer. However when it came time to prostrate I was surprised to find him next to me on the ground prostrating. I thought that the guy fell facefirst out of his chair and felt sorry for him because I wasn't going to interrupt my prayer to help him up. Yet then after the prostration he pushed himself up back into the chair. For the next 3 units he did the same thing, lunging out of his chair to throw his body on the ground to prostrate then using his arm muscles to push himself back into his chair for the other parts of the prayer. He was just as fast at prostrating and getting up as I was despite him only having 1 leg to do it. It was a remarkable feat that the man did not have to do, islamically he had a legitimate excuse/concession to sit in his chair but he didn't. This was because he loves prostrating in prayer so much that he does it even though only having one leg means he's not required to do it, he chooses to do so out of love for Allah and because praying the best way he can and prostrating as Muhammad pbuh taught us to do makes him happy. Therefore to anyone who claims that they "can't pray like Muslims do because they can't prostrate on the ground" I just ask them flat out if they truly can't or if they just don't want to because I've prayed next to a man who only had one leg but he still prostrated on the ground 8 separate times in the span of a few minutes. So if he can do it, I think many others could too, if they wanted to do so. Likewise for those who claim they "can't stop sinning" I ask them if they want to. Because if you truly want to stop sinning then you will, it might be hard and take a long time to achieve that goal with lots of practice but if you intend something then it will happen. This is because deeds are according to your intentions, if you really intend to do something you will and if you intend not to do something you won't. It's rarely ever about can or can't, it's if you want to then your desires will cause you to find a way to make it happen and God will help. Just consider the power of your desires, if a tiny part of you wants to sin then how often does that tiny desire get you into sinful trouble? If a tiny desire to sin can result in sin then imagine what a pure intention and major desire to do good or avoid evil will result in? The only way you can fail to accomplish your goal when you have a pure good intention is if God wanted something better for you.

This applies to praying on time in the masjid. If one wants to pray in the masjid they will find a way to do it. If it was their last day of life a Muslim would make sure they prayed on time in the masjid if possible, so they can make the time but because they forget their appointment with death they misprioritize while they are alive and say they can't when they just can't prioritize prayer as important as they should. The correct priority is pray-work-play, some don't put prayer first because they don't view God as most important in their life. If God was the most important thing in their life then prayer would be the most important activity in their day. Since prayer is the most important thing one can do in a day, if a person truly can't pray to their Maker then they are either in a coma, insane, a child, with a legitimate excuse such as a menstruating woman or they can't do nothing at all. If you can't pray you can't play. If you can't pray you can't work. You can pray if you can't work, study or play but you can't do any of those extra things if you can't pray. If God commands you to pray that means you can do it, to say you can't is to say God is wrong. Whereas for one to say or think that God is wrong is to disbelieve in God. Prayer is not just something God says you "have to do" it's an actual appointment with the Creator of the Universe. When Allah instructs men to pray in the masjid at certain times that is a personal appointment with every single man which God has set up specially to take place in God's own house. Yes people can pray most anywhere but when God picks a particular place for the special appointment called prayer then you don't want to "call in from a different location". While prayer is commonly known to be the oldest type of wireless connection, the masjids have the best reception. The daily Islamic prayers are all more important than doctors appointments, job interviews, playing in championship games, and even taking an exam in school. The prayer at a masjid is literally a meeting between the created and the Creator where direct communication takes place in the spot specially created by the Creator for this special meeting. The true believer values these meetings as the highlight of their day and everything else in life revolves around their prayers or appointments. Work, School and Play is interrupted for prayer because it's an appointment with God and you don't delay or disappoint God when God makes an appointment with you. Sometimes when people invite me to stuff or if I'm at an event and it's time to pray then instead of saying I'm going to pray at the masjid, if I think they will give me a hassle, I tell them I have an appointment to go to and they encourage me to get to it soon. They don't need to know it's an appointment to worship God, all that matters is I make it. I don't lie, I just don't risk my appointment with God if I think telling them it's with God will risk it, other times the pride I have in the divine appointment causes me to be happy to share the good news. Other times I don't tolerate their intolerance and when people try to delay my prayer or change it's location I say, "*Who do you think you are? On one side there is the Creator of the Universe telling me to pray at X time in Z location and on the other side there is you telling me not to. One has created me, the world, paradise and hell and you have done what? Just, how arrogant, selfish and foolish can you be? Where do you get the audacity? How dare you?! How dare you? You were joking right? Did you actually think you were more important than me praying to God? Are you mentally insane?*" It's really sad because if you tell people " I have an appointment" they let you interrupt everything and go, but if you tell them you are going to worship God and pray then some types of people will be negative not realizing that worshipping God is the most important type of appointment in your life.

Muslims are busy people, God cares about us so much we have 5 appointments with him everyday, which God himself made with us and rewards us for going to on time with eagerness and our full attention. It's not a hassle to worship God 5 times a day, it's a joy to pray. That's why we come early to prayer and avoid being late. Even though coming late is better than never, we still don't want to show up late to our appointment with the Creator of the Universe. Muslims will actually come late to their own wedding in order to pray on time. While most non-Muslims view their wedding as their most important moment in life, Muslims view each obligatory prayer as more important than their wedding. So since work, school and life is interrupted for weddings Muslims have no regrets or hesitation to pray on time in masjids. We reserve our time to pray to God and God reserves and improves a spot for us in paradise. Our work, school and play is scheduled around our daily prayers. If a Muslim is playing in a championship game they will stop playing and sit out of the final game-deciding play in order to pray because the true champion is the one who prays to Allah, not the one who plays, studies, or works. Those people who neglect their appointments with God are insulting God. Likewise when you have an appointment with God, you make sure your cellphone is off so it doesn't interrupt or negatively impact the interaction. For example if a priest were to have his phone go off in the middle of a church service while giving his sermon, or when doing a baptism, marrying people, hearing confession or giving out communion then it would be a huge scandal. Muslims would feel it's even more scandalous for a cellphone to go off during their daily prayers, even if it just vibrates. The same applies to anything that distracts/disrupts a Muslim from their prayer whether it's external or internal. If one is caused to delay or neglect their prayer by either not praying in the masjid or being distracted when praying due to thoughts of their investments, career or other worldly matters this is lamentable. For every type of income opportunity whether one is a investor, entrepreneur, employer or laborer one's profession and/or income source should not distract them or negatively affect or limit their prayer. Salat is more important than one's salary and we should be thinking about our salat when at work rather than thinking about our work when in salat. Only true danger distracts a Muslim during prayer and sometimes if they are extra pious

they don't even feel danger or pain when praying.
Imam Bukhari was once stung by a wasp 17 times
while praying, people only realized he had been
stung after he was done leading them in prayer and
he asked if there was something on his back so they
checked under his shirt and the wasp was
discovered with 17 stings. Another Muslim named
Abaad ibn Bishr was once shot with 3 arrows by a
non-Muslim whilst performing a voluntary prayer
when guarding the Muslim army camp at night, but
he didn't stop praying to ask for help because he
was enjoying reciting the Quran too much to stop.
He simply removed each arrow and kept on
praying without stopping. When asked the reason
he didn't sound the alarm, Abaad explained he only
alerted the others by praying aloud when he did
because he was afraid that if he was killed during
his prayer then the enemy might kill more Muslims
due to him not making a noise when he got shot 3
times. Abaad didn't think getting shot multiple
times was enough of a reason to disrupt his Islamic
prayer. Why? Because Abaad said praying the way
Muhammad pbuh taught him while reciting the
Quran was simply too much fun to stop. Prayer in
Islam is not a mere activity it is an interactive event
wherein the Creator of the Universe interacts with

Muslims throughout the day personally responding to us throughout the various phases of our prayer. Muslims don't have to wait until death to meet God, we meet God every time we pray since our salat is interactive. A Muslim's prayer is a meeting with God where God has given us a special script to say. Since our God manages to meet us when we pray we do our best to meet him on-time in the designated meeting place to pray. For one who knows they are created to pray that's what they do throughout the day, when and where and how God says to. A life neglecting the islamic prayers is not a life worth living. Muslims need not pray for success because praying in the prophetic manner with sincerity is the true success in life. Regardless of your material wealth and health the wise one measures their health and wealth in terms of their spiritual life. Praying in the masjid for Muslim men is so important that some of them won't even marry a woman whose father or brothers don't pray their 5 obligatory prayers on-time in the masjid every day. This is because if a Muslim man isn't responsible enough to pray to Allah in Allah's house 5 times a day then he isn't really qualified to raise righteous children. If a man can't take care of his prayers he can't take care of a kid, so some Muslim men refuse to even marry Muslim women who's Muslim father doesn't pray 5 times a day in the masjid. This doesn't just have to do with the father but the woman herself as well, because if a Muslim woman doesn't care enough about her Muslim father to ensure that he is praying his 5 daily prayers in the masjid then she isn't going to care about her children's prayers either nor her husband. The same applies to her brothers if she doesn't motivate her Muslim brothers to pray in the masjid 5 times a day she isn't a good sister and if she isn't a good sister/daughter she won't be a good wife or mother. Likewise I wouldn't want my child's Muslim grandfather to be someone who doesn't pray in the masjid, nor would I want my child's Muslim uncles to be those who neglect prayers at the masjid. Some Muslims even go so far as to apply this to a woman's grandfather and prefer to marry a woman whose grandfather prays 5 times a day in the masjid. Of course for people who are non-Muslim then become Muslim the expectations are different for their family and even themselves(to some extent, since living life without Islam can cause the transition to a full Islamic life to take some time and serious effort and struggle), but born and raised Muslims are traditionally held to a much higher standard. This is because prayer in God's house is so important for Muslim men. Being a parent or spouse is a position of leadership and Islamically the companions of Muhammad pbuh would never allow Muslim men who didn't pray their 5 daily prayers in the masjid to occupy any position of leadership. Unfortunately standards have declined in the modern era, but the prophetic standard is that Muslim men who don't pray their 5 daily prayers in the masjid aren't qualified for positions of leadership, whether big or small. And I don't know of any type of leadership that is more important than that of being a parent, except perhaps leading people in prayer. For a Muslim nothing is comparable to prayer and we don't compromise it for anything or anyone at anytime unless God's prophets did so; such as in the case of a military battle there is a prayer style Muslims pray that differs somewhat from the regular one. This is because your prayer is only profitable if it's done the prophetic way. The truly sick and poor people are those who neglect their prayers. To worship Allah is the best ship one can sail on and a Muslim doesn't sell their salat for anything. Prayers involve words but words don't do our prayers justice. The only flaw in praying is that our prayers can be imperfect. To pray a perfect prayer is the key to paradise and happiness, to neglect prayers or do them in a way other than how your prophet taught is the key to hell both on earth and after death. Angels pray to God correctly on time in the place God loves them to pray, while devils fail in that regard. Which are you like? The most prized gift in life is to pray to your Creator. It's only to help you pray that God gave you health and wealth and created the entire Universe, so you could enjoy a perfect prayer to your Lord in the manner his prophets taught. If you're doing it right praying is more enjoyable than playing. Prayer if done correctly prevents you from sinning, so if you are a sinner then something in your prayers are deficient. God's houses (masjids) aren't just some "special spiritual place of worship", the true friends of God view every masjid as their best friend's house.

Before a human is even born they are completely helpless in the womb, entirely dependent upon nutrition from their mother, without which they wouldn't survive, did we worry? Next after birth we can't walk, talk or even clean ourselves still being totally dependent on others to feed, clean and clothe us, did we worry? As a toddler we were able to express ourselves and move yet even then we were dependent, because we could be starving and have food right in front of us yet be unable to access it because we couldn't open the container, did we worry? Eventually as an adult when we are finally strong, smart and able, with the ability to find work, build and earn, then we start to worry about how we're going to put food on our plate and pay the bills and what if you get hurt or can't get a job or this or that or what? Do you think you survived this long because of yourself or the help of others? It was none but Allah that made food come your way, gave you the ability to digest it and receive nutrition from it as well as helping it exit the body afterwards, without staying inside you forever. Ask anyone who ever suffered constipation how grateful they are to be able to digest and have the waste exit their body. Many people in the world today have lost the ability to urinate and defecate and need artificial help to do so or else they would be in unbearable pain retaining everything they eat or drink. We didn't worry when we were at our weakest so why do we worry now? Truly we have been deceived by the deceiver Satan, who makes us forget our sustainer and threatens us with poverty. Even in poverty the worst case scenario is that you become so poor that you die, but you are going to die anyways, even then you would still be provided with life once again by Allah and resurrected. Don't worry about the material things in life. The worst that can happen as a result of poverty is guaranteed to happen to everybody anyways. Allah has already made our lives much easier than those who came before us in comparison with the rest of humanity throughout all time. Even the poorest amongst us has it good compared to what the richest ones in the past had. The kings of old don't even come close to having what our modern peasant has. Yet we dare to complain or worry about money? Money cannot buy you health, happiness, sleep, contentment, family, tranquility, righteous children, good friends or patience. Why do we place so much emphasis on money when it is momentary? Money is phony, it is nothing but a temporary unit of exchange. The real currency on the day of resurrection will be the good deeds one has accumulated and all the bad deeds will be a debt that must be repaid if it is not forgiven. This life is like a field with which to plant seeds of goodness in, the harvest and reward comes after the resurrection. Unfortunately some people don't spend their life sowing seeds of good deeds, but spend it on immediate gratification like the farmer who spends their seed money on candy. It tastes sweet while in their mouth, but when it is time for harvest and the sweet sensations are long gone and forgotten, nothing will be left except the bitter taste of regret because they never prepared for the next season. Prepare for your next life, don't be worried about this one. No matter what you do, everything you accumulate here will leave you and you will leave this life behind. Nothing here is ours, it is just temporarily leased. Our home is in one of two places, heaven or hell. We will move to one of those places sooner than we realize it. There will be no rent, property taxes or expenses for the palaces in paradise and they last forever with no maintenance required as they're eternally upgraded. That sounds expensive and it is, so we must work hard for the afterlife now in order to afford the payment on the home in paradise, it must be paid in full before our death. This earth we live in now is temporary so stop worrying about it. The more Allah allots to you the more Satan will try to distract you with it to be ungrateful. Don't ever worship *"the Almighty Dollar"*, instead you should worship the Almighty Creator of everything. God even provides health and sustenance to Satan despite his wickedness, so surely God will provide for you, so you'd be an enormous idiot to do financial sins or worry about money. The money doesn't care about you, so why would you care about the money? People will say *"well I don't know if I'm going to have enough money 10 years from now"* yet nobody even told them they'll be alive 10 seconds from now. Millions of people have had an opportunity to give in charity and they didn't because they worried that they will "need the money" next decade, next year or next week and after keeping their money they ended up dying that same day. Then they regret not giving the money in charity for eternity, because it could have saved them from punishment for their sins or got them a gazillion extra mansions in paradise. They always wish they had known they were going to die so that they could have spent it in charity, well I'm telling you right now in capital letters in case you didn't know "YOU ARE GOING TO DIE SOON!" Others think that they have to save everything for their heirs to survive on after they die. Whereas the best thing to do for your heirs is to guide them to worship their Creator. Let's say you die poor and your heirs are poor pious believers. Do you think God isn't going to provide for them? Surely he will!

On the other hand lets say you die rich and your heirs are sinful or disbelievers who use the money you left them disobeying God and living sinfully or in disbelief. That would make you responsible for all those sins they do since you provided them the means to sin. So if your heirs are good then God will provide for them and if they're bad then you don't want to be punished for them using the money you leave them sinfully anyways. If you really cared for your heirs you'd teach them to worship God since believers and disbelievers don't inherit from each other anyways. I'm not saying to give everything in charity, but realistically most of us save more money than we should and earn more than we need. The best inheritance you can give is knowledge and the correct example, while ideally investing your money in ongoing charity projects so that way one gets the largest return on investment possible. God gives you life everyday, so why don't you give charity everyday? If your money isn't spent in charity then you most likely wasted it. God will ask you about every atom of wealth, and punish you or reward you for how you earned and spent it. Don't you want to tell God you spent in charity and get rewarded for it forever? God loves to give generously to those who give generously.

The more you give the more God will give you to give so you can be given more to give. While the less you give the less God will give you.

Treat work as though it's like the toilet. You go there when you need to, do your best and that's all, you have no business spending your life there. If don't want to work as much just don't spend as much, if you simply decrease your expenditure by 50% then you'll either have 50% more money or you can spend 50% less time working for money. After work you should spend time for religion and if you need to take breaks to relax and recharge to become a better worshipper then that's ok. Although remember that Allah has ordered us to worship him when we're not working too. So don't give your human boss more effort than you do the boss of the universe. The human bosses are really our coworkers who have the same job of worshipping God as we do and it's well known that to be successful in one's job and get promoted if the boss is pleased then you will succeed, even if all your coworkers hate you. Whereas if you please all your coworkers and displease your boss(God) then you won't succeed no matter what. Just as you'd give priority to the CEO's rules over your manager's, one must give priority to God's rules over your human bosses'. Just as a manager can't give you or deprive you of payment without the CEO allowing it, none can give you or deprive you of wealth/ health without God's permission. Worshipping Allah is a full-time job with permanent benefits. Every other job is temporary with temporary benefits. Of course working to provide for family is a form of worship in and of itself if the person has the right intention, especially if one works in order to have more money to give in charity, having such intentions can make every second you spend working your job count as a way of worshipping God. Although a man having intercourse with his wife in order to remove his desire for illegal sexual acts, bond with and please one's spouse can also be considered a way of worshipping God if it's done in the manner God is pleased with and not in a way God has forbidden. Yet if a man had intercourse with his wife for the majority of his life without focusing on learning his religion, then what would we say of such a person? Eating can also be worship too, if you're eating the right things the right way for the right reasons, but if someone was eating 24/7 that would be a problem. They would be worshipping Mr. Tongue or Mr. Stomach, with their temples being the dining tables and toilets.

Likewise don't work too much for this worldly life because soon you will leave it all behind and be brought to account for everything you enjoyed in this life. Being a workaholic is sinful, as is being a shopaholic. In the afterlife all of us will wish we were poor, ill and oppressed in this life so we don't have to answer for all the bounties we received. Poor believers enter paradise 500 years before rich believers do. Throughout his life Muhammad pbuh even asked for the favor of living and dying poor because God has such a better and more favorable attitude and treatment towards them in this life and the next. Too often we make the same mistake as the ant. If you study the ant you will find it to be incredibly blessed and gifted able to do amazing things that cause one to marvel at it. Many can even carry humongous leaves many times their size and intelligently use such leaves in a multitude of ways, for food, shelter, status, livelihood and even travel across water or cracks upon their leaf with which their life on earth would be drastically different if not impossible without using certain qualities or quantities of leaves. However at the end of the ant's journey it arrives at it's home, a tiny hole in the ground. Yet despite doing so much to obtain and maintain it's leaf, which it carried with it for a lengthy amount of time the ant cannot take it's leaf with it into it's home (hole in the ground). Thus when all is said and done, the ant came out of a tiny hole in the beginning of it's day and it returns to a tiny hole in the ground at the end of it's day with no material possessions at all, despite spending so much time and effort worrying about, acquiring and maintaining it's worldly leaf. Essentially most ants make a poor investment in leaves every day of their life, despite knowing their end result is a hole in the ground, just as it is for us. Therefore we should invest more in the next life that we'll soon be experiencing forever, without end; even if it's at the expense of this life/leaf. An investment in the afterlife is infinitely more rewarding than any investment made in this life. Focus on your house in paradise rather than maintaining your property on earth that will end up inherited by someone else anyway. The ant can take more into their hole in the ground than we can take with us into our grave. Especially in regards to worldly abodes people spend so foolishly. I personally know people who buy dirt or mulch on an annual basis because they don't like the natural dirt on the ground where they live, so to make it easier to plant their flowers they literally buy dirt despite millions throughout the world starving. What would God's prophets say to them? Yet don't we all buy dirt? Afterall we were made from dirt, and we turn back into dirt when we die, so while chastising those who buy literal dirt, theologically we are none the wiser because we spoil soil. By which I mean we spoil the base soil-like substance of ourselves at the expense of our soul and shall regret our neglectful extravagance when we see what we've prepared for our home beneath the soil. Our faces will indeed be grave on the day when we realize we didn't spend on things that would benefit us in the grave. Focus on the future after-life it will soon become the present, whereas the present time has already become the past by the time you finished reading this sentence. Remember that before God passes his sentence on us we will be asked what we spent our youth, wealth, health, life and time on. Also keep in mind God has scheduled 5 appointments with you every day and your Creator will ask you about each one he invited you to. So make your meetings(prayers) with God in this life great and you will have a great meeting with God in court after you die. You not only have time to worship God 5 times a day but you can worship God 24 hours a day. To worship God is to have the intention to please God by doing what he wants you to do at every particular moment in your life sincerely for his sake alone according to his prophets instructions for how to live your life. If you intend to please God and are doing what God wants you to do in the way God wants you to do it every second, then by God's definition you would be worshipping him every second. Just adopt the prophetic intention and do the prophetic actions. To worship God is a type of mentality, intention and lifestyle. Your God made you to worship him every second, and you can. If you think you can't or find it hard then ask God to help you. Asking God to help you worship him is a type of worship too. You can worship God every second for the rest of your life. But do you want to? And will you? Satan will try to stop you. Every second there is a battle to see if you worship God or don't. Whereas the special help given to the blessed worshippers to achieve their noble objective is attained through Patience and Prayer.

Quranic Ayat on Patience and/or Prayer

Quran 2:3

ٱلَّذِينَ يُؤْمِنُونَ بِٱلْغَيْبِ وَيُقِيمُونَ ٱلصَّلَوٰةَ وَمِمَّا رَزَقْنَـٰهُمْ يُنفِقُونَ

Who believe in the Ghaib[unseen] and perform As-Salât (Prayer), and spend out of what we have provided for them [i.e. give Zakât, spend on themselves, their parents, their children, their wives, etc., and also give charity to the poor and also in Allâh's Cause - Jihâd,]. (3)

Quran 2:43-45

وَأَقِيمُواْ ٱلصَّلَوٰةَ وَءَاتُواْ ٱلزَّكَوٰةَ وَٱرْكَعُواْ مَعَ ٱلرَّٰكِعِينَ ﴿٤٣﴾ أَتَأْمُرُونَ ٱلنَّاسَ بِٱلْبِرِّ وَتَنسَوْنَ أَنفُسَكُمْ وَأَنتُمْ تَتْلُونَ ٱلْكِتَـٰبَ أَفَلَا تَعْقِلُونَ ﴿٤٤﴾ وَٱسْتَعِينُواْ بِٱلصَّبْرِ وَٱلصَّلَوٰةِ وَإِنَّهَا لَكَبِيرَةٌ إِلَّا عَلَى ٱلْخَـٰشِعِينَ ﴿٤٥﴾

And perform As-Salât (Prayer), and give Zakât, and bow down (or submit yourselves with obedience to Allâh) along with Ar¬Raki'ûn. (43) Enjoin you Al-Birr (piety and righteousness and each and every act of obedience to Allâh) on the people and you forget (to practise it) yourselves, while you recite the Scripture! Have you then no sense? (44) And seek help in patience and As-

Salât (the prayer) and truly it is extremely heavy and hard except for Al-Khâshi'ûn [i.e. the true believers in Allâh - those who obey Allâh with full submission, fear much from His Punishment, and believe in His Promise (Paradise,) and in His Warnings (Hell,)]. (45)

Quran 2:83

وَإِذْ أَخَذْنَا مِيثَاقَ بَنِى إِسْرَأَءِيلَ لَا تَعْبُدُونَ إِلَّا ٱللَّهَ وَبِٱلْوَ ٰلِدَيْنِ إِحْسَانًا وَذِى ٱلْقُرْبَىٰ وَٱلْيَتَـٰمَىٰ وَٱلْمَسَـٰكِينِ وَقُولُواْ لِلنَّاسِ حُسْنًا وَأَقِيمُواْ ٱلصَّلَوٰةَ وَءَاتُواْ ٱلزَّكَوٰةَ ثُمَّ تَوَلَّيْتُمْ إِلَّا قَلِيلًا مِّنكُمْ وَأَنتُم مُّعْرِضُونَ

And (remember) when We took a covenant from the Children of Israel, (saying): Worship none but Allâh (Alone) and be dutiful and good to parents, and to kindred, and to orphans and Al-Masâkîn (the poor), and speak good to people [i.e. enjoin righteousness and forbid evil, and say the truth about Muhammad], and perform As-Salât (Prayers), and give Zakât. Then you slid back, except a few of you, while you are backsliders. (83)

Quran 2:110

وَأَقِيمُواْ ٱلصَّلَوٰةَ وَءَاتُواْ ٱلزَّكَوٰةَ وَمَا تُقَدِّمُواْ لِأَنفُسِكُم مِّنْ خَيْرٍ تَجِدُوهُ عِندَ ٱللَّهِ إِنَّ ٱللَّهَ بِمَا تَعْمَلُونَ بَصِيرٌ

And perform As-Salât (Prayers), and give Zakât, and whatever of good (deeds that Allâh loves) you send forth

*for yourselves before you, you shall find it with Allâh.
Certainly, Allâh is All-Seer of what you do. (110)*

Quran 2:142-145

﴿سَيَقُولُ ٱلسُّفَهَآءُ مِنَ ٱلنَّاسِ مَا وَلَّىٰهُمْ عَن قِبْلَتِهِمُ ٱلَّتِى كَانُوا۟ عَلَيْهَا قُل لِّلَّهِ ٱلْمَشْرِقُ وَٱلْمَغْرِبُ يَهْدِى مَن يَشَآءُ إِلَىٰ صِرَٰطٍ مُّسْتَقِيمٍ (١٤٢) وَكَذَٰلِكَ جَعَلْنَٰكُمْ أُمَّةً وَسَطًا لِّتَكُونُوا۟ شُهَدَآءَ عَلَى ٱلنَّاسِ وَيَكُونَ ٱلرَّسُولُ عَلَيْكُمْ شَهِيدًا وَمَا جَعَلْنَا ٱلْقِبْلَةَ ٱلَّتِى كُنتَ عَلَيْهَآ إِلَّا لِنَعْلَمَ مَن يَتَّبِعُ ٱلرَّسُولَ مِمَّن يَنقَلِبُ عَلَىٰ عَقِبَيْهِ وَإِن كَانَتْ لَكَبِيرَةً إِلَّا عَلَى ٱلَّذِينَ هَدَى ٱللَّهُ وَمَا كَانَ ٱللَّهُ لِيُضِيعَ إِيمَٰنَكُمْ إِنَّ ٱللَّهَ بِٱلنَّاسِ لَرَءُوفٌ رَّحِيمٌ (١٤٣) قَدْ نَرَىٰ تَقَلُّبَ وَجْهِكَ فِى ٱلسَّمَآءِ فَلَنُوَلِّيَنَّكَ قِبْلَةً تَرْضَىٰهَا فَوَلِّ وَجْهَكَ شَطْرَ ٱلْمَسْجِدِ ٱلْحَرَامِ وَحَيْثُ مَا كُنتُمْ فَوَلُّوا۟ وُجُوهَكُمْ شَطْرَهُ وَإِنَّ ٱلَّذِينَ أُوتُوا۟ ٱلْكِتَٰبَ لَيَعْلَمُونَ أَنَّهُ ٱلْحَقُّ مِن رَّبِّهِمْ وَمَا ٱللَّهُ بِغَٰفِلٍ عَمَّا يَعْمَلُونَ (١٤٤) وَلَئِنْ أَتَيْتَ ٱلَّذِينَ أُوتُوا۟ ٱلْكِتَٰبَ بِكُلِّ ءَايَةٍ مَّا تَبِعُوا۟ قِبْلَتَكَ وَمَآ أَنتَ بِتَابِعٍ قِبْلَتَهُمْ وَمَا بَعْضُهُم بِتَابِعٍ قِبْلَةَ بَعْضٍ وَلَئِنِ ٱتَّبَعْتَ أَهْوَآءَهُم مِّن بَعْدِ مَا جَآءَكَ مِنَ ٱلْعِلْمِ إِنَّكَ إِذًا لَّمِنَ ٱلظَّٰلِمِينَ (١٤٥)﴾

*The fools among the people (pagans, hypocrites, and
Jews) will say, "What has turned them (Muslims) from
their Qiblah [prayer direction (towards Jerusalem)] to
which they were used to face in prayer." Say, "To Allâh
belong both, east and the west. He guides whom He wills*

to a Straight Way." (142) Thus We have made you [true Muslims - real believers of Islâmic Monotheism, true followers of Prophet Muhammad and his Sunnah (legal ways)], a (just) (and the best) nation, that you be witnesses over mankind and the Messenger (Muhammad) be a witness over you. And We made the Qiblah (prayer direction towards Jerusalem) which you used to face, only to test those who followed the Messenger (Muhammad) from those who would turn on their heels (i.e. disobey the Messenger). Indeed it was great (heavy) except for those whom Allâh guided. And Allâh would never make your faith (prayers) to be lost (i.e. your prayers offered towards Jerusalem). Truly, Allâh is full of kindness, the Most Merciful towards mankind. (143) Verily! We have seen the turning of your (Muhammad's) face towards the heaven. Surely, We shall turn you to a Qiblah (prayer direction) that shall please you, so turn your face in the direction of Al-Masjid- Al-Harâm (at Makkah). And wheresoever you people are, turn your faces (in prayer) in that direction. Certainly, the people who were given the Scriptures (i.e. Jews and the Christians) know well that, that (your turning towards the direction of the Ka'bah at Makkah in prayers) is the truth from their Lord. And Allâh is not unaware of what they do. (144) And even if you were to bring to the people of the Scripture (Jews and Christians) all the Ayât (proofs, evidences, verses, lessons, signs,

revelations, etc.), they would not follow your Qiblah
(prayer direction), nor are you going to follow their
Qiblah (prayer direction). And they will not follow each
other's Qiblah (prayer direction). Verily, if you follow
their desires after that which you have received of
knowledge (from Allâh), then indeed you will be one of
the Zâlimûn (polytheists, wrong-doers.) (145)

Quran 2:153

يَٰٓأَيُّهَا ٱلَّذِينَ ءَامَنُوا۟ ٱسْتَعِينُوا۟ بِٱلصَّبْرِ وَٱلصَّلَوٰةِ إِنَّ ٱللَّهَ مَعَ
ٱلصَّٰبِرِينَ

O you who believe! Seek help in patience and As-Salât
(the prayer). Truly! Allâh is with As-Sâbirun (the
patient.) (153)

Quran 2:155-157

وَلَنَبْلُوَنَّكُم بِشَىْءٍ مِّنَ ٱلْخَوْفِ وَٱلْجُوعِ وَنَقْصٍ مِّنَ ٱلْأَمْوَٰلِ
وَٱلْأَنفُسِ وَٱلثَّمَرَٰتِ وَبَشِّرِ ٱلصَّٰبِرِينَ (١٥٥) ٱلَّذِينَ إِذَآ
أَصَٰبَتْهُم مُّصِيبَةٌ قَالُوٓا۟ إِنَّا لِلَّهِ وَإِنَّآ إِلَيْهِ رَٰجِعُونَ
(١٥٦) أُو۟لَٰٓئِكَ عَلَيْهِمْ صَلَوَٰتٌ مِّن رَّبِّهِمْ وَرَحْمَةٌ وَأُو۟لَٰٓئِكَ هُمُ
ٱلْمُهْتَدُونَ (١٥٧)

And certainly, We shall test you with something of fear,
hunger, loss of wealth, lives and fruits, but give glad
tidings to As-Sâbirun (the patient) (155) Who, when
afflicted with calamity, say: "Truly! To Allâh we belong

and truly, to Him we shall return." (156) They are those on whom are the Salawât (i.e. who are blessed) from their Lord, and (they are those who) receive His Mercy, and it is they who are the guided-ones. (157)

Quran 2:238-239

حَـٰفِظُواْ عَلَى ٱلصَّلَوَٰتِ وَٱلصَّلَوٰةِ ٱلْوُسْطَىٰ وَقُومُواْ لِلَّهِ قَـٰنِتِينَ (٢٣٨) فَإِنْ خِفْتُمْ فَرِجَالاً أَوْ رُكْبَانًا فَإِذَآ أَمِنتُمْ فَٱذْكُرُواْ ٱللَّهَ كَمَا عَلَّمَكُم مَّا لَمْ تَكُونُواْ تَعْلَمُونَ (٢٣٩)

Guard strictly (five obligatory) As¬Salawât (the prayers) especially the middle Salât (i.e. the best prayer ¬ 'Asr). And stand before Allâh with obedience [and do not speak to others during the Salât (prayers)]. (238)And if you fear (an enemy), perfrom Salât (pray) on foot or riding. And when you are in safety, offer the Salât (prayer) in the manner He has taught you, which you knew not (before). (239)

Quran 2:277

إِنَّ ٱلَّذِينَ ءَامَنُواْ وَعَمِلُواْ ٱلصَّـٰلِحَـٰتِ وَأَقَامُواْ ٱلصَّلَوٰةَ وَءَاتَوُاْ ٱلزَّكَوٰةَ لَهُمْ أَجْرُهُمْ عِندَ رَبِّهِمْ وَلَا خَوْفٌ عَلَيْهِمْ وَلَا هُمْ يَحْزَنُونَ

Truly those who believe, and do deeds of righteousness, and perform As-Salât (Prayers), and give Zakât, they will have their reward with their Lord. On them shall be no fear, nor shall they grieve. (277)

Quran 3:16-17

ٱلَّذِينَ يَقُولُونَ رَبَّنَآ إِنَّنَآ ءَامَنَّا فَٱغْفِرْ لَنَا ذُنُوبَنَا وَقِنَا عَذَابَ ٱلنَّارِ (١٦) ٱلصَّـٰبِرِينَ وَٱلصَّـٰدِقِينَ وَٱلْقَـٰنِتِينَ وَٱلْمُنفِقِينَ وَٱلْمُسْتَغْفِرِينَ بِٱلْأَسْحَارِ (١٧)

Those who say: "Our Lord! We have indeed believed, so forgive us our sins and save us from the punishment of the Fire." (16) (They are) those who are patient, those who are true (in Faith, words, and deeds), and obedient with sincere devotion in worship to Allâh. Those who spend [give the Zakât and alms in the Way of Allâh] and those who pray and beg Allâh's Pardon in the last hours of the night. (17)

Quran 3:142

أَمْ حَسِبْتُمْ أَن تَدْخُلُواْ ٱلْجَنَّةَ وَلَمَّا يَعْلَمِ ٱللَّهُ ٱلَّذِينَ جَـٰهَدُواْ مِنكُمْ وَيَعْلَمَ ٱلصَّـٰبِرِينَ

Do you think that you will enter Paradise before Allâh tests those of you who fought (in His Cause) and (also) tests those who are As-Sâbirun (the patient)? (142)

Quran 3:200

يَـٰٓأَيُّهَا ٱلَّذِينَ ءَامَنُوا۟ ٱصْبِرُوا۟ وَصَابِرُوا۟ وَرَابِطُوا۟ وَٱتَّقُوا۟
ٱللَّهَ لَعَلَّكُمْ تُفْلِحُونَ

O you who believe! Endure and be more patient, and guard your territory by stationing army units permanently at the places from where the enemy can attack you, and fear Allâh, so that you may be successful. (200)

Quran 4:43

يَـٰٓأَيُّهَا ٱلَّذِينَ ءَامَنُوا۟ لَا تَقْرَبُوا۟ ٱلصَّلَوٰةَ وَأَنتُمْ سُكَـٰرَىٰ حَتَّىٰ
تَعْلَمُوا۟ مَا تَقُولُونَ وَلَا جُنُبًا إِلَّا عَابِرِى سَبِيلٍ حَتَّىٰ تَغْتَسِلُوا۟
وَإِن كُنتُم مَّرْضَىٰٓ أَوْ عَلَىٰ سَفَرٍ أَوْ جَآءَ أَحَدٌ مِّنكُم مِّنَ
ٱلْغَآئِطِ أَوْ لَـٰمَسْتُمُ ٱلنِّسَآءَ فَلَمْ تَجِدُوا۟ مَآءً فَتَيَمَّمُوا۟ صَعِيدًا
طَيِّبًا فَٱمْسَحُوا۟ بِوُجُوهِكُمْ وَأَيْدِيكُمْ إِنَّ ٱللَّهَ كَانَ عَفُوًّا
غَفُورًا

O you who believe! Approach not As¬Salât (the prayer) when you are in a drunken state until you know (the meaning) of what you utter, nor when you are in a state of Janâba, (i.e. in a state of sexual impurity and have not yet taken a bath) except when travelling on the road (without enough water, or just passing through a mosque), till you wash your whole body. And if you are ill, or on a journey, or one of you comes after answering the call of nature, or you have been in contact with women (by sexual relations) and you find no water, perform Tayammum with clean earth and rub therewith your faces and hands (Tayammum). Truly, Allâh is Ever Oft¬Pardoning, Oft¬Forgiving. (43)

Quran 4:77

أَلَمْ تَرَ إِلَى ٱلَّذِينَ قِيلَ لَهُمْ كُفُّوٓاْ أَيْدِيَكُمْ وَأَقِيمُواْ ٱلصَّلَوٰةَ وَءَاتُواْ ٱلزَّكَوٰةَ فَلَمَّا كُتِبَ عَلَيْهِمُ ٱلْقِتَالُ إِذَا فَرِيقٌ مِّنْهُمْ يَخْشَوْنَ ٱلنَّاسَ كَخَشْيَةِ ٱللهِ أَوْ أَشَدَّ خَشْيَةً وَقَالُواْ رَبَّنَا لِمَ كَتَبْتَ عَلَيْنَا ٱلْقِتَالَ لَوْلَا أَخَّرْتَنَا إِلَىٰ أَجَلٍ قَرِيبٍ قُلْ مَتَٰعُ ٱلدُّنْيَا قَلِيلٌ وَٱلْأَخِرَةُ خَيْرٌ لِّمَنِ ٱتَّقَىٰ وَلَا تُظْلَمُونَ فَتِيلاً

Have you not seen those who were told to hold back their hands (from fighting) and perform As-Salât (Prayers), and give Zakât but when the fighting was ordained for them, behold! a section of them fear men as they fear Allâh or even more. They say: "Our Lord! Why have you ordained for us fighting? Would that You had granted us respite for a short period?" Say: "Short is the enjoyment of this world. The Hereafter is (far) better for him who fears Allâh, and you shall not be dealt with unjustly even equal to a scalish thread in the long slit of a date-stone. (77)

Quran 4:101-103

وَإِذَا ضَرَبْتُمْ فِى ٱلْأَرْضِ فَلَيْسَ عَلَيْكُمْ جُنَاحٌ أَن تَقْصُرُواْ مِنَ ٱلصَّلَوٰةِ إِنْ خِفْتُمْ أَن يَفْتِنَكُمُ ٱلَّذِينَ كَفَرُوٓاْ إِنَّ ٱلْكَٰفِرِينَ كَانُواْ

لَكُمْ عَدُوًّا مُّبِينًا (١٠١) وَإِذَا كُنتَ فِيهِمْ فَأَقَمْتَ لَهُمُ ٱلصَّلَوٰةَ
فَلْتَقُمْ طَآئِفَةٌ مِّنْهُم مَّعَكَ وَلْيَأْخُذُوٓاْ أَسْلِحَتَهُمْ فَإِذَا سَجَدُواْ
فَلْيَكُونُواْ مِن وَرَآئِكُمْ وَلْتَأْتِ طَآئِفَةٌ أُخْرَىٰ لَمْ يُصَلُّواْ
فَلْيُصَلُّواْ مَعَكَ وَلْيَأْخُذُواْ حِذْرَهُمْ وَأَسْلِحَتَهُمْ وَدَّ ٱلَّذِينَ كَفَرُواْ
لَوْ تَغْفُلُونَ عَنْ أَسْلِحَتِكُمْ وَأَمْتِعَتِكُمْ فَيَمِيلُونَ عَلَيْكُم مَّيْلَةً
وَٰحِدَةً وَلَا جُنَاحَ عَلَيْكُمْ إِن كَانَ بِكُمْ أَذًى مِّن مَّطَرٍ أَوْ كُنتُم
مَّرْضَىٰٓ أَن تَضَعُوٓاْ أَسْلِحَتَكُمْ وَخُذُواْ حِذْرَكُمْ إِنَّ ٱللَّهَ أَعَدَّ
لِلْكَٰفِرِينَ عَذَابًا مُّهِينًا (١٠٢) فَإِذَا قَضَيْتُمُ ٱلصَّلَوٰةَ فَٱذْكُرُواْ
ٱللَّهَ قِيَٰمًا وَقُعُودًا وَعَلَىٰ جُنُوبِكُمْ فَإِذَا ٱطْمَأْنَنتُمْ فَأَقِيمُواْ
ٱلصَّلَوٰةَ إِنَّ ٱلصَّلَوٰةَ كَانَتْ عَلَى ٱلْمُؤْمِنِينَ كِتَٰبًا مَّوْقُوتًا
(١٠٣)

And when you (Muslims) travel in the land, there is no
sin on you if you shorten As-Salât (the prayer) if you fear
that the disbelievers may put you in trial (attack you
etc.), verily, the disbelievers are ever unto you open
enemies. (101) When you (O Messenger Muhammad)
are among them, and lead them in As-Salât (the prayer),
let one party of them stand up [in Salât (prayer)] with
you taking their arms with them; when they finish their
prostrations, let them take their positions in the rear and
let the other party come up which have not yet prayed,
and let them pray with you taking all the precautions and
bearing arms. Those who disbelieve wish, if you were
negligent of your arms and your baggage, to attack you

in a single rush, but there is no sin on you if you put away your arms because of the inconvenience of rain or because you are ill, but take every precaution for yourselves. Verily, Allâh has prepared a humiliating torment for the disbelievers. (102) When you have finished As-Salât (the prayer - congregational), remember Allâh standing, sitting down, and (lying down) on your sides, but when you are free from danger, perform As-Salât (Iqâmat¬as¬ Salât). Verily, As-Salât (the prayer) is enjoined on the believers at fixed hours. (103)

Quran 4:142

إِنَّ ٱلْمُنَٰفِقِينَ يُخَٰدِعُونَ ٱللَّهَ وَهُوَ خَٰدِعُهُمْ وَإِذَا قَامُوٓاْ إِلَى ٱلصَّلَوٰةِ قَامُواْ كُسَالَىٰ يُرَآءُونَ ٱلنَّاسَ وَلَا يَذْكُرُونَ ٱللَّهَ إِلَّا قَلِيلاً

Verily, the hypocrites seek to deceive Allâh, but it is He Who deceives them. And when they stand up for As-Salât (the prayer), they stand with laziness and to be seen of men, and they do not remember Allâh but little. (142)

Quran 4:162

لَّٰكِنِ ٱلرَّٰسِخُونَ فِى ٱلْعِلْمِ مِنْهُمْ وَٱلْمُؤْمِنُونَ يُؤْمِنُونَ بِمَآ أُنزِلَ إِلَيْكَ وَمَآ أُنزِلَ مِن قَبْلِكَ وَٱلْمُقِيمِينَ ٱلصَّلَوٰةَ

وَٱلْمُؤْتُونَ ٱلزَّكَوٰةَ وَٱلْمُؤْمِنُونَ بِٱللَّهِ وَٱلْيَوْمِ ٱلْأَخِرِ أُوْلَـٰٓئِكَ سَنُؤْتِيهِمْ أَجْرًا عَظِيمًا

But those among them who are well-grounded in knowledge, and the believers, believe in what has been sent down to you (Muhammad) and what was sent down before you, and those who perform As-Salât (Prayers), and give Zakât and believe in Allâh and in the Last Day, it is they to whom We shall give a great reward. (162)

Quran 5:12

وَلَقَدْ أَخَذَ ٱللَّهُ مِيثَـٰقَ بَنِىٓ إِسْرَٰٓءِيلَ وَبَعَثْنَا مِنْهُمُ ٱثْنَىْ عَشَرَ نَقِيبًا وَقَالَ ٱللَّهُ إِنِّى مَعَكُمْ لَئِنْ أَقَمْتُمُ ٱلصَّلَوٰةَ وَءَاتَيْتُمُ ٱلزَّكَوٰةَ وَءَامَنتُم بِرُسُلِى وَعَزَّرْتُمُوهُمْ وَأَقْرَضْتُمُ ٱللَّهَ قَرْضًا حَسَنًا لَّأُكَفِّرَنَّ عَنكُمْ سَيِّـَٔاتِكُمْ وَلَأُدْخِلَنَّكُمْ جَنَّـٰتٍ تَجْرِى مِن تَحْتِهَا ٱلْأَنْهَـٰرُ فَمَن كَفَرَ بَعْدَ ذَٰلِكَ مِنكُمْ فَقَدْ ضَلَّ سَوَآءَ ٱلسَّبِيلِ

Indeed Allâh took the covenant from the Children of Israel (Jews), and We appointed twelve leaders among them. And Allâh said: "I am with you if you perform As-Salât (Prayers) and give Zakât and believe in My Messengers; honour and assist them, and lend a good loan to Allâh. Verily, I will expiate your sins and admit you to Gardens under which rivers flow (in Paradise). But if any of you after this, disbelieved, he has indeed gone astray from the Straight Path." (12)

Quran 5:55

إِنَّمَا وَلِيُّكُمُ ٱللَّهُ وَرَسُولُهُ وَٱلَّذِينَ ءَامَنُواْ ٱلَّذِينَ يُقِيمُونَ ٱلصَّلَوٰةَ وَيُؤْتُونَ ٱلزَّكَوٰةَ وَهُمْ رَاكِعُونَ

Verily, your Walî (Protector or Helper) is none other than Allâh, His Messenger, and the believers, - those who perform As-Salât (Prayers), and give Zakât, and they are Rakiun (those who bow down or submit themselves with obedience to Allâh in prayer). (55)

Quran 5:58

وَإِذَا نَادَيْتُمْ إِلَى ٱلصَّلَوٰةِ ٱتَّخَذُوهَا هُزُوًا وَلَعِبًا ذَٰلِكَ بِأَنَّهُمْ قَوْمٌ لَّا يَعْقِلُونَ

And when you proclaim the call for As-Salât [call for the prayer (Adhân)], they take it (but) as a mockery and fun; that is because they are a people who understand not. (58)

Quran 6:34

وَلَقَدْ كُذِّبَتْ رُسُلٌ مِّن قَبْلِكَ فَصَبَرُواْ عَلَىٰ مَا كُذِّبُواْ وَأُوذُواْ حَتَّىٰ أَتَىٰهُمْ نَصْرُنَا وَلَا مُبَدِّلَ لِكَلِمَٰتِ ٱللَّهِ وَلَقَدْ جَآءَكَ مِن نَّبَإِىْ ٱلْمُرْسَلِينَ

Verily, (many) Messengers were denied before you (O Muhammad), but with patience they bore the denial, and they were hurt, till Our Help reached them, and none can alter the Words (Decisions) of Allâh. Surely there has reached you the information (news) about the Messengers (before you) (34)

Quran 6:71-72

قُلْ أَنَدْعُواْ مِن دُونِ ٱللَّهِ مَا لَا يَنفَعُنَا وَلَا يَضُرُّنَا وَنُرَدُّ عَلَىٰٓ أَعْقَابِنَا بَعْدَ إِذْ هَدَىٰنَا ٱللَّهُ كَٱلَّذِى ٱسْتَهْوَتْهُ ٱلشَّيَٰطِينُ فِى ٱلْأَرْضِ حَيْرَانَ لَهُۥٓ أَصْحَٰبٌ يَدْعُونَهُۥٓ إِلَى ٱلْهُدَى ٱئْتِنَا قُلْ إِنَّ هُدَى ٱللَّهِ هُوَ ٱلْهُدَىٰ وَأُمِرْنَا لِنُسْلِمَ لِرَبِّ ٱلْعَٰلَمِينَ (٧١) وَأَنْ أَقِيمُواْ ٱلصَّلَوٰةَ وَٱتَّقُوهُ وَهُوَ ٱلَّذِىٓ إِلَيْهِ تُحْشَرُونَ (٧٢)

Say: "Shall we invoke others besides Allâh (false deities), that can do us neither good nor harm, and shall we turn back on our heels after Allâh has guided us (to true Monotheism)? - like one whom the Shayâtîn (devils) have made to go astray, in the land in confusion, his companions calling him to guidance (saying): 'Come to us.'" Say: "Verily, Allâh's Guidance is the only guidance, and we have been commanded to submit (ourselves) to the Lord of the 'Alamîn (mankind, jinn and all that exists); (71) And to perform As-Salât (Prayers)", and to be obedient to Allâh and fear Him, and it is He to Whom you shall be gathered. (72)

Quran 6:92

وَهَٰذَا كِتَٰبٌ أَنزَلْنَٰهُ مُبَارَكٌ مُّصَدِّقُ ٱلَّذِى بَيْنَ يَدَيْهِ
وَلِتُنذِرَ أُمَّ ٱلْقُرَىٰ وَمَنْ حَوْلَهَآ وَٱلَّذِينَ يُؤْمِنُونَ بِٱلْءَاخِرَةِ
يُؤْمِنُونَ بِهِۦۖ وَهُمْ عَلَىٰ صَلَاتِهِمْ يُحَافِظُونَ

*And this (the Qur'ân) is a blessed Book which We have
sent down, confirming (the revelations) which came
before it, so that you may warn the Mother of Towns (i.e.
Makkah) and all those around it. Those who believe in the
Hereafter believe in it (the Qur'ân), and they are
constant in guarding their Salât (prayers). (92)*

Quran 7:128

قَالَ مُوسَىٰ لِقَوْمِهِ ٱسْتَعِينُوا۟ بِٱللَّهِ وَٱصْبِرُوٓا۟ۖ إِنَّ ٱلْأَرْضَ لِلَّهِ
يُورِثُهَا مَن يَشَآءُ مِنْ عِبَادِهِۦۖ وَٱلْعَٰقِبَةُ لِلْمُتَّقِينَ

*Mûsa (Moses) said to his people: "Seek help in Allâh and
be patient. Verily, the earth is Allâh's. He gives it as a
heritage to whom He wills of His slaves, and the (blessed)
end is for the Muttaqûn (pious)." (128)*

Quran 8:2-4

إِنَّمَا ٱلْمُؤْمِنُونَ ٱلَّذِينَ إِذَا ذُكِرَ ٱللَّهُ وَجِلَتْ قُلُوبُهُمْ وَإِذَا تُلِيَتْ
عَلَيْهِمْ ءَايَٰتُهُۥ زَادَتْهُمْ إِيمَٰنًا وَعَلَىٰ رَبِّهِمْ يَتَوَكَّلُونَ (٢) ٱلَّذِينَ
يُقِيمُونَ ٱلصَّلَوٰةَ وَمِمَّا رَزَقْنَٰهُمْ يُنفِقُونَ (٣) أُو۟لَٰٓئِكَ هُمُ
ٱلْمُؤْمِنُونَ حَقًّاۚ لَهُمْ دَرَجَٰتٌ عِندَ رَبِّهِمْ وَمَغْفِرَةٌ وَرِزْقٌ كَرِيمٌ
(٤)

The believers are only those who, when Allâh is mentioned, feel a fear in their hearts and when His Verses (this Qur'ân) are recited unto them, they (i.e. the Verses) increase their Faith; and they put their trust in their Lord (Alone); (2) Who perform As-Salât (Prayers) and spend out of that We have provided them. (3) It is they who are the believers in truth. For them are grades of dignity with their Lord, and Forgiveness and a generous provision (Paradise). (4)

Quran 8:35

وَمَا كَانَ صَلَاتُهُمْ عِندَ ٱلْبَيْتِ إِلَّا مُكَآءً وَتَصْدِيَةً فَذُوقُواْ ٱلْعَذَابَ بِمَا كُنتُمْ تَكْفُرُونَ

Their Salât (prayer) at the House (of Allâh, i.e. the Ka'bah at Makkah) was nothing but whistling and clapping of hands. Therefore taste the punishment because you used to disbelieve (35)

Quran 8:65-66

يَـٰٓأَيُّهَا ٱلنَّبِىُّ حَرِّضِ ٱلْمُؤْمِنِينَ عَلَى ٱلْقِتَالِ إِن يَكُن مِّنكُمْ عِشْرُونَ صَـٰبِرُونَ يَغْلِبُواْ مِائَتَيْنِ وَإِن يَكُن مِّنكُم مِّائَةٌ يَغْلِبُوٓاْ أَلْفًا مِّنَ ٱلَّذِينَ كَفَرُواْ بِأَنَّهُمْ قَوْمٌ لَّا يَفْقَهُونَ (٦٥) ٱلْـَٔـٰنَ خَفَّفَ ٱللَّهُ عَنكُمْ وَعَلِمَ أَنَّ فِيكُمْ ضَعْفًا فَإِن يَكُن مِّنكُم مِّائَةٌ صَابِرَةٌ يَغْلِبُواْ مِائَتَيْنِ وَإِن يَكُن مِّنكُمْ أَلْفٌ يَغْلِبُوٓاْ أَلْفَيْنِ بِإِذْنِ ٱللَّهِ وَٱللَّهُ مَعَ ٱلصَّـٰبِرِينَ (٦٦)

O Prophet (Muhammad)! Urge the believers to fight. If there are twenty steadfast persons amongst you, they will overcome two hundred, and if there be a hundred steadfast persons they will overcome a thousand of those who disbelieve, because they (the disbelievers) are people who do not understand. (65) Now Allâh has lightened your (task), for He knows that there is weakness in you. So if there are of you a hundred steadfast persons, they shall overcome two hundreds, and if there are a thousand of you, they shall overcome two thousand with the Leave of Allâh. And Allâh is with As-Sâbirûn (the patient). (66)

Quran 9:11

فَإِن تَابُوا۟ وَأَقَامُوا۟ ٱلصَّلَوٰةَ وَءَاتَوُا۟ ٱلزَّكَوٰةَ فَإِخْوَٰنُكُمْ فِى ٱلدِّينِ ۗ وَنُفَصِّلُ ٱلْءَايَٰتِ لِقَوْمٍ يَعْلَمُونَ

But if they repent, perform As-Salât (Prayers) and give Zakât, then they are your brethren in religion. (In this way) We explain the Ayât (proofs, evidences, verses, lessons, signs, revelations, etc.) in detail for a people who know. (11)

Quran 9:18

إِنَّمَا يَعْمُرُ مَسَٰجِدَ ٱللَّهِ مَنْ ءَامَنَ بِٱللَّهِ وَٱلْيَوْمِ ٱلْءَاخِرِ وَأَقَامَ ٱلصَّلَوٰةَ وَءَاتَى ٱلزَّكَوٰةَ وَلَمْ يَخْشَ إِلَّا ٱللَّهَ ۖ فَعَسَىٰٓ أُو۟لَٰٓئِكَ أَن يَكُونُوا۟ مِنَ ٱلْمُهْتَدِينَ

The Mosques of Allâh shall be maintained only by those who believe in Allâh and the Last Day; perform As-Salât (Prayers), and give Zakât and fear none but Allâh. It is they who are on true guidance. (18)

Quran 9:54

وَمَا مَنَعَهُمْ أَن تُقْبَلَ مِنْهُمْ نَفَقَٰتُهُمْ إِلَّا أَنَّهُمْ كَفَرُوا۟ بِٱللَّهِ وَبِرَسُولِهِۦ وَلَا يَأْتُونَ ٱلصَّلَوٰةَ إِلَّا وَهُمْ كُسَالَىٰ وَلَا يُنفِقُونَ إِلَّا وَهُمْ كَٰرِهُونَ

And nothing prevents their contributions from being accepted from them except that they disbelieved in Allâh and in His Messenger (Muhammad); and that they came not to As-Salât (the prayer) except in a lazy state; and that they offer not contributions but unwillingly. (54)

Quran 10:87

وَأَوْحَيْنَآ إِلَىٰ مُوسَىٰ وَأَخِيهِ أَن تَبَوَّءَا لِقَوْمِكُمَا بِمِصْرَ بُيُوتًا وَٱجْعَلُوا۟ بُيُوتَكُمْ قِبْلَةً وَأَقِيمُوا۟ ٱلصَّلَوٰةَ وَبَشِّرِ ٱلْمُؤْمِنِينَ

And We revealed to Mûsa (Moses) and his brother (saying): "Provide dwellings for your people in Egypt, and make your dwellings as places for your worship, and perform As-Salât (Prayers), and give glad tidings to the believers." (87)

Quran 11:9-11

وَلَئِنْ أَذَقْنَا ٱلْإِنسَٰنَ مِنَّا رَحْمَةً ثُمَّ نَزَعْنَٰهَا مِنْهُ إِنَّهُ لَيَـُٔوسٌ كَفُورٌ (٩) وَلَئِنْ أَذَقْنَٰهُ نَعْمَآءَ بَعْدَ ضَرَّآءَ مَسَّتْهُ لَيَقُولَنَّ ذَهَبَ ٱلسَّيِّـَٔاتُ عَنِّىٓ إِنَّهُ لَفَرِحٌ فَخُورٌ (١٠) إِلَّا ٱلَّذِينَ صَبَرُوا۟ وَعَمِلُوا۟ ٱلصَّٰلِحَٰتِ أُو۟لَٰٓئِكَ لَهُم مَّغْفِرَةٌ وَأَجْرٌ كَبِيرٌ (١١)

And if We give man a taste of Mercy from Us, and then withdraw it from him, verily! he is despairing, ungrateful. (9) But if We let him taste good (favour) after evil (poverty and harm) has touched him, he is sure to say: "Ills have departed from me." Surely, he is exultant, and boastful (ungrateful to Allâh). (10) Except those who show patience and do righteous good deeds, those: theirs will be forgiveness and a great reward (Paradise). (11)

Quran 11:87

قَالُوا۟ يَٰشُعَيْبُ أَصَلَوٰتُكَ تَأْمُرُكَ أَن نَّتْرُكَ مَا يَعْبُدُ ءَابَآؤُنَآ أَوْ أَن نَّفْعَلَ فِىٓ أَمْوَٰلِنَا مَا نَشَٰٓؤُا۟ إِنَّكَ لَأَنتَ ٱلْحَلِيمُ ٱلرَّشِيدُ

They said: "O Shu'aib! Does your Salât (prayer) command that we give up what our fathers used to worship, or that we give up doing what we like with our property? Verily, you are the forbearer, right-minded!" (They said this sarcastically). (87)

Quran 11:114-115

وَأَقِمِ ٱلصَّلَوٰةَ طَرَفَيِ ٱلنَّهَارِ وَزُلَفًا مِّنَ ٱلَّيْلِ إِنَّ ٱلْحَسَنَٰتِ يُذْهِبْنَ ٱلسَّيِّئَاتِ ذَٰلِكَ ذِكْرَىٰ لِلذَّٰكِرِينَ (١١٤) وَٱصْبِرْ فَإِنَّ ٱللَّهَ لَا يُضِيعُ أَجْرَ ٱلْمُحْسِنِينَ (١١٥)

And perform As-Salât (Prayers), at the two ends of the day and in some hours of the night [i.e. the five compulsory Salât (prayers)]. Verily, the good deeds remove the evil deeds (i.e. small sins). That is a reminder (an advice) for the mindful (those who accept advice). (114) And be patient; verily, Allâh wastes not the reward of the good-doers. (115)

Quran 12:18

وَجَآءُو عَلَىٰ قَمِيصِهِ بِدَمٍ كَذِبٍ قَالَ بَلْ سَوَّلَتْ لَكُمْ أَنْفُسُكُمْ أَمْرًا فَصَبْرٌ جَمِيلٌ وَٱللَّهُ ٱلْمُسْتَعَانُ عَلَىٰ مَا تَصِفُونَ

And they brought his shirt stained with false blood. He said: "Nay, but your ownselves have made up a tale. So (for me) patience is most fitting. And it is Allâh (Alone) Whose help can be sought against that (lie) which you describe." (18)

Quran 12:83

قَالَ بَلْ سَوَّلَتْ لَكُمْ أَنْفُسُكُمْ أَمْرًا فَصَبْرٌ جَمِيلٌ عَسَى ٱللَّهُ أَن يَأْتِيَنِى بِهِمْ جَمِيعًا إِنَّهُ هُوَ ٱلْعَلِيمُ ٱلْحَكِيمُ

He [Ya'qûb (Jacob)] said: "Nay, but your ownselves have beguiled you into something. So patience is most fitting (for me). Maybe Allâh will bring them (back) all to me. Truly He! only He is All-Knowing, All-Wise." (83)

Quran 12:90

قَالُوٓاْ أَءِنَّكَ لَأَنتَ يُوسُفُۖ قَالَ أَنَاْ يُوسُفُ وَهَـٰذَآ أَخِىۖ قَدْ مَنَّ ٱللَّهُ عَلَيْنَآۖ إِنَّهُۥ مَن يَتَّقِ وَيَصْبِرْ فَإِنَّ ٱللَّهَ لَا يُضِيعُ أَجْرَ ٱلْمُحْسِنِينَ

They said: "Are you indeed Yûsuf (Joseph)?" He said: "I am Yûsuf (Joseph), and this is my brother (Benjamin). Allâh has indeed been gracious to us. Verily, he who fears Allâh with obedience to Him (by abstaining from sins and evil deeds, and by performing righteous good deeds), and is patient, then surely, Allâh makes not the reward of the Muhsinûn (good-doers) to be lost." (90)

Quran 13:22-24

وَٱلَّذِينَ صَبَرُواْ ٱبْتِغَآءَ وَجْهِ رَبِّهِمْ وَأَقَامُواْ ٱلصَّلَوٰةَ وَأَنفَقُواْ مِمَّا رَزَقْنَـٰهُمْ سِرًّا وَعَلَانِيَةً وَيَدْرَءُونَ بِٱلْحَسَنَةِ ٱلسَّيِّئَةَ أُوْلَـٰٓئِكَ لَهُمْ عُقْبَى ٱلدَّارِ (٢٢) جَنَّـٰتُ عَدْنٍ يَدْخُلُونَهَا وَمَن صَلَحَ مِنْ ءَابَآئِهِمْ وَأَزْوَٰجِهِمْ وَذُرِّيَّـٰتِهِمْۖ وَٱلْمَلَـٰٓئِكَةُ يَدْخُلُونَ عَلَيْهِم مِّن كُلِّ بَابٍ (٢٣) سَلَـٰمٌ عَلَيْكُم بِمَا صَبَرْتُمْۚ فَنِعْمَ عُقْبَى ٱلدَّارِ (٢٤)

And those who remain patient, seeking their Lord's Countenance, perform As-Salât (Prayers), and spend out of that which We have bestowed on them, secretly and openly, and combat evil with good, for such there is a

good end; (22) 'Adn (Eden) Paradise (everlasting
Gardens), which they shall enter and (also) those who
acted righteously from among their fathers, and their
wives, and their offspring. And angels shall enter unto
them from every gate (saying): (23) "Salâmun 'Alaikum
(peace be upon you) for that you persevered in patience!
Excellent indeed is the final home!" (24)

Quran 14:31

قُل لِّعِبَادِىَ ٱلَّذِينَ ءَامَنُواْ يُقِيمُواْ ٱلصَّلَوٰةَ وَيُنفِقُواْ مِمَّا رَزَقْنَـٰهُمْ
سِرًّا وَعَلَانِيَةً مِّن قَبْلِ أَن يَأْتِىَ يَوْمٌ لَّا بَيْعٌ فِيهِ وَلَا
خِلَـٰلٌ

Say (O Muhammad) to 'Ibâdî (My slaves) who have
believed, that they should perform As-Salât (Prayers),
and spend in charity out of the sustenance We have given
them, secretly and openly, before the coming of a Day on
which there will be neither mutual bargaining nor
befriending. (31)

Quran 14:37

رَبَّنَآ إِنِّىٓ أَسْكَنتُ مِن ذُرِّيَّتِى بِوَادٍ غَيْرِ ذِى زَرْعٍ عِندَ بَيْتِكَ
ٱلْمُحَرَّمِ رَبَّنَا لِيُقِيمُواْ ٱلصَّلَوٰةَ فَٱجْعَلْ أَفْئِدَةً مِّنَ ٱلنَّاسِ تَهْوِىٓ
إِلَيْهِمْ وَٱرْزُقْهُم مِّنَ ٱلثَّمَرَٰتِ لَعَلَّهُمْ يَشْكُرُونَ

"O our Lord! I have made some of my offspring to dwell
in an uncultivable valley by Your Sacred House (the

Ka'bah at Makkah); in order, O our Lord, that they may perform As-Salât (Prayers), so fill some hearts among men with love towards them, and (O Allâh) provide them with fruits so that they may give thanks.(37)

Quran 14:40

رَبِّ ٱجْعَلْنِى مُقِيمَ ٱلصَّلَوٰةِ وَمِن ذُرِّيَّتِىْ رَبَّنَا وَتَقَبَّلْ دُعَآءِ

"O my Lord! Make me one who performs As-Salât (Prayers), and (also) from my offspring, our Lord! And accept my invocation. (40)

Quran 16:110

ثُمَّ إِنَّ رَبَّكَ لِلَّذِينَ هَاجَرُواْ مِنْ بَعْدِ مَا فُتِنُواْ ثُمَّ جَـٰهَدُواْ وَصَبَرُوٓاْ إِنَّ رَبَّكَ مِنۢ بَعْدِهَا لَغَفُورٌ رَّحِيمٌ

Then, verily! Your Lord for those who emigrated after they had been put to trials and thereafter strove hard and fought (for the Cause of Allâh) and were patient, verily, your Lord afterward is, Oft-Forgiving, Most Merciful. (110)

Quran 16:126-127

وَإِنْ عَاقَبْتُمْ فَعَاقِبُواْ بِمِثْلِ مَا عُوقِبْتُم بِهِۦ وَلَئِن صَبَرْتُمْ لَهُوَ خَيْرٌ لِّلصَّـٰبِرِينَ (١٢٦) وَٱصْبِرْ وَمَا صَبْرُكَ إِلَّا بِٱللَّهِ وَلَا تَحْزَنْ عَلَيْهِمْ وَلَا تَكُ فِى ضَيْقٍ مِّمَّا يَمْكُرُونَ (١٢٧)

And if you punish (your enemy, O you believers in the Oneness of Allâh), then punish them with the like of that with which you were afflicted. But if you endure patiently, verily, it is better for As-Sâbirun (the patient). (126) And endure you patiently (O Muhammad), your patience is not but from Allâh. And grieve not over them (polytheists and pagans), and be not distressed because of what they plot. (127)

Quran 17:78-79

أَقِمِ ٱلصَّلَوٰةَ لِدُلُوكِ ٱلشَّمْسِ إِلَىٰ غَسَقِ ٱلَّيْلِ وَقُرْءَانَ ٱلْفَجْرِ إِنَّ قُرْءَانَ ٱلْفَجْرِ كَانَ مَشْهُودًا (٧٨) وَمِنَ ٱلَّيْلِ فَتَهَجَّدْ بِهِۦ نَافِلَةً لَّكَ عَسَىٰٓ أَن يَبْعَثَكَ رَبُّكَ مَقَامًا مَّحْمُودًا (٧٩)

Perform As¬Salât (Prayers) from mid-day till the darkness of the night (i.e. the Zuhr, 'Asr, Maghrib, and 'Ishâ' prayers), and recite the Qur'ân in the early dawn (i.e. the morning prayer). Verily, the recitation of the Qur'ân in the early dawn is ever witnessed (attended by the angels in charge of mankind of the day and the night). (78) And in some parts of the night (also) offer the Salât (prayer) with it (i.e. recite the Qur'an in the prayer), as an additional prayer (Tahajjud optional prayer - Nawâfil) for you (O Muhammad). It may be that your Lord will raise you to Maqâm Mahmûd (a station of praise and glory, i.e. the honour of intercession on the Day of Resurrection). (79)

Quran 18:28

وَٱصْبِرْ نَفْسَكَ مَعَ ٱلَّذِينَ يَدْعُونَ رَبَّهُم بِٱلْغَدَوٰةِ وَٱلْعَشِىِّ يُرِيدُونَ وَجْهَهُۥ وَلَا تَعْدُ عَيْنَاكَ عَنْهُمْ تُرِيدُ زِينَةَ ٱلْحَيَوٰةِ ٱلدُّنْيَا وَلَا تُطِعْ مَنْ أَغْفَلْنَا قَلْبَهُۥ عَن ذِكْرِنَا وَٱتَّبَعَ هَوَىٰهُ وَكَانَ أَمْرُهُۥ فُرُطًا

And keep yourself (O Muhammad) patiently with those who call on their Lord (i.e. your companions who remember their Lord with glorification, praising in prayers, and other righteous deeds) morning and afternoon, seeking His Face, and let not your eyes overlook them, desiring the pomp and glitter of the life of the world; and obey not him whose heart We have made heedless of Our Remembrance, and who follows his own lusts and whose affair (deeds) has been lost. (28)

Quran 18:67-69

قَالَ إِنَّكَ لَن تَسْتَطِيعَ مَعِىَ صَبْرًا (٦٧) وَكَيْفَ تَصْبِرُ عَلَىٰ مَا لَمْ تُحِطْ بِهِۦ خُبْرًا (٦٨) قَالَ سَتَجِدُنِىَ إِن شَآءَ ٱللَّهُ صَابِرًا وَلَآ أَعْصِى لَكَ أَمْرًا (٦٩)

He (Khidr) said: "Verily! You will not be able to have patience with me! (67) "And how can you have patience about a thing which you know not?" (68) Mûsa (Moses) said: "If Allâh wills, you will find me patient, and I will not disobey you in aught." (69)

Quran 18:72

قَالَ أَلَمْ أَقُلْ إِنَّكَ لَن تَسْتَطِيعَ مَعِىَ صَبْرًا

He (Khidr) said: "Did I not tell you, that you would not be able to have patience with me?" (72)

Quran 18:75

قَالَ أَلَمْ أَقُل لَّكَ إِنَّكَ لَن تَسْتَطِيعَ مَعِىَ صَبْرًا ۞

(Khidr) said: "Did I not tell you that you can have no patience with me?" (75)

Quran 18:78

قَالَ هَـٰذَا فِرَاقُ بَيْنِى وَبَيْنِكَ سَأُنَبِّئُكَ بِتَأْوِيلِ مَا لَمْ تَسْتَطِع عَّلَيْهِ صَبْرًا

(Khidr) said: "This is the parting between me and you, I will tell you the interpretation of (those) things over which you were unable to hold patience (78)

Quran 19:31

وَجَعَلَنِى مُبَارَكًا أَيْنَ مَا كُنتُ وَأَوْصَـٰنِى بِٱلصَّلَوٰةِ وَٱلزَّكَوٰةِ مَا دُمْتُ حَيًّا

"And He has made me blessed wheresoever I be, and has enjoined on me Salât (prayer), and Zakât, as long as I live." (31)

Quran 19:55

وَكَانَ يَأْمُرُ أَهْلَهُ بِٱلصَّلَوٰةِ وَٱلزَّكَوٰةِ وَكَانَ عِندَ رَبِّهِ مَرْضِيًّا

And he used to enjoin on his family and his people As-Salât (the prayers) and the Zakât, and his Lord was pleased with him. (55)

Quran 19:59

فَخَلَفَ مِنْ بَعْدِهِمْ خَلْفٌ أَضَاعُوا۟ ٱلصَّلَوٰةَ وَٱتَّبَعُوا۟ ٱلشَّهَوَٰتِ فَسَوْفَ يَلْقَوْنَ غَيًّا

Then, there has succeeded them a posterity who have given up As-Salât (the prayers) [i.e. made their Salât (prayers) to be lost, either by not offering them or by not offering them perfectly or by not offering them in their proper fixed times] and have followed lusts. So they will be thrown in Hell. (59)

Quran 20:14

إِنَّنِىٓ أَنَا ٱللَّهُ لَآ إِلَٰهَ إِلَّآ أَنَا۠ فَٱعْبُدْنِى وَأَقِمِ ٱلصَّلَوٰةَ لِذِكْرِىٓ

"Verily! I am Allâh! Lâ ilâha illa Ana (none has the right to be worshipped but I), so worship Me, and perform As-Salât (Prayers) for My Remembrance. (14)

Quran 20:130

فَٱصْبِرْ عَلَىٰ مَا يَقُولُونَ وَسَبِّحْ بِحَمْدِ رَبِّكَ قَبْلَ طُلُوعِ
ٱلشَّمْسِ وَقَبْلَ غُرُوبِهَا وَمِنْ ءَانَآيِٕ ٱلَّيْلِ فَسَبِّحْ وَأَطْرَافَ
ٱلنَّهَارِ لَعَلَّكَ تَرْضَىٰ

*So bear patiently what they say, and glorify the praises of
your Lord before the rising of the sun, and before its
setting, and during some hours of the night, and at the
ends of the day (an indication for the five compulsory
congregational prayers), that you may become pleased
with the reward which Allâh shall give you. (130)*

Quran 20:132

وَأْمُرْ أَهْلَكَ بِٱلصَّلَوٰةِ وَٱصْطَبِرْ عَلَيْهَا لَا نَسْـَٔلُكَ رِزْقًا
نَّحْنُ نَرْزُقُكَ وَٱلْعَـٰقِبَةُ لِلتَّقْوَىٰ

*And enjoin As-Salât (the prayer) on your family, and be
patient in offering them [i.e. the Salât (prayers)]. We ask
not of you a provision; We provide for you. And the good
end (i.e. Paradise) is for the Muttaqûn (pious and
righteous). (132)*

Quran 21:73

وَجَعَلْنَـٰهُمْ أَئِمَّةً يَهْدُونَ بِأَمْرِنَا وَأَوْحَيْنَآ إِلَيْهِمْ فِعْلَ ٱلْخَيْرَٰتِ
وَإِقَامَ ٱلصَّلَوٰةِ وَإِيتَآءَ ٱلزَّكَوٰةِ وَكَانُوا۟ لَنَا عَـٰبِدِينَ

*And We made them leaders, guiding (mankind) by Our
Command, and We revealed them the doing of good*

deeds, performing Salât (Prayers), and the giving of Zakât and of Us (Alone) they were the worshippers. (73)

Quran 21:85

وَإِسْمَـٰعِيلَ وَإِدْرِيسَ وَذَا ٱلْكِفْلِ ۖ كُلٌّ مِّنَ ٱلصَّـٰبِرِينَ

And (remember) Isma'îl (Ishmael), and Idris (Enoch) and Dhul-Kifl (Isaiah), all were from among As-Sâbirun (the patient). (85)

Quran 22:35

ٱلَّذِينَ إِذَا ذُكِرَ ٱللَّهُ وَجِلَتْ قُلُوبُهُمْ وَٱلصَّـٰبِرِينَ عَلَىٰ مَآ أَصَابَهُمْ وَٱلْمُقِيمِى ٱلصَّلَوٰةِ وَمِمَّا رَزَقْنَـٰهُمْ يُنفِقُونَ

Whose hearts are filled with fear when Allâh is mentioned; and As-Sabirun [the patient); and who perform As-Salât (Prayers), and who spend (in Allâh's Cause) out of what We have provided them. (35)

Quran 22:41

ٱلَّذِينَ إِن مَّكَّنَّـٰهُمْ فِى ٱلْأَرْضِ أَقَامُوا۟ ٱلصَّلَوٰةَ وَءَاتَوُا۟ ٱلزَّكَوٰةَ وَأَمَرُوا۟ بِٱلْمَعْرُوفِ وَنَهَوْا۟ عَنِ ٱلْمُنكَرِ ۗ وَلِلَّهِ عَـٰقِبَةُ ٱلْأُمُورِ

Those who, if We give them power in the land, (they) enjoin Iqamat-as-Salât. [i.e. to perform the five compulsory congregational Salât (prayers) (the males in mosques)], to pay the Zakât and they enjoin Al-Ma'rûf (i.e. Islâmic Monotheism and all that Islâm orders one to do), and forbid Al-Munkar (i.e. disbelief, polytheism and all that Islâm has forbidden). And with Allâh rests the end of (all) matters (of creatures). (41)

Quran 23:2

ٱلَّذِينَ هُمْ فِى صَلَاتِهِمْ خَٰشِعُونَ

Those who offer their Salât (prayers) with all solemnity and full submissiveness. (2)

Quran 23:9

وَٱلَّذِينَ هُمْ عَلَىٰ صَلَوَٰتِهِمْ يُحَافِظُونَ

And those who strictly guard their (five compulsory congregational) Salawât (prayers) (at their fixed stated hours). (9)

Quran 24:37

رِجَالٌ لَّا تُلْهِيهِمْ تِجَٰرَةٌ وَلَا بَيْعٌ عَن ذِكْرِ ٱللَّهِ وَإِقَامِ ٱلصَّلَوٰةِ وَإِيتَآءِ ٱلزَّكَوٰةِ يَخَافُونَ يَوْمًا تَتَقَلَّبُ فِيهِ ٱلْقُلُوبُ وَٱلْأَبْصَٰرُ

Men whom neither trade nor sale (business) diverts them from the Remembrance of Allâh (with heart and tongue), nor from performing As¬Salât (Prayers), nor from giving the Zakât. They fear a Day when hearts and eyes will be overturned (out of the horror of the torment of the Day of Resurrection). (37)

Quran 24:41

أَلَمْ تَرَ أَنَّ ٱللَّهَ يُسَبِّحُ لَهُ مَن فِى ٱلسَّمَٰوَٰتِ وَٱلْأَرْضِ وَٱلطَّيْرُ صَٰٓفَّٰتٍ ۖ كُلٌّ قَدْ عَلِمَ صَلَاتَهُ وَتَسْبِيحَهُ ۗ وَٱللَّهُ عَلِيمٌ بِمَا يَفْعَلُونَ

See you not that Allâh, He it is Whom glorify whosoever is in the heavens and the earth, and the birds with wings out-spread (in their flight)? Of each one He (Allâh) knows indeed his Salât (prayer) and his glorification, [or everyone knows his Salât (prayer) and his glorification], and Allâh is All-Aware of what they do. (41)

Quran 24:56

وَأَقِيمُوا۟ ٱلصَّلَوٰةَ وَءَاتُوا۟ ٱلزَّكَوٰةَ وَأَطِيعُوا۟ ٱلرَّسُولَ لَعَلَّكُمْ تُرْحَمُونَ

And perform As¬Salât (Prayers), and give Zakât and obey the Messenger (Muhammad) that you may receive mercy (from Allâh). (56)

Quran 27:3

ٱلَّذِينَ يُقِيمُونَ ٱلصَّلَوٰةَ وَيُؤْتُونَ ٱلزَّكَوٰةَ وَهُم بِٱلْءَاخِرَةِ هُمْ يُوقِنُونَ

Those who perform As¬Salât (Prayers) and give Zakât and they believe with certainty in the Hereafter (resurrection, recompense of their good and bad deeds, Paradise and Hell). (3)

Quran 28:80

وَقَالَ ٱلَّذِينَ أُوتُوا ٱلْعِلْمَ وَيْلَكُمْ ثَوَابُ ٱللَّهِ خَيْرٌ لِّمَنْ ءَامَنَ وَعَمِلَ صَلِحًا وَلَا يُلَقَّهَا إِلَّا ٱلصَّبِرُونَ

But those who had been given (religious) knowledge said: "Woe to you! The Reward of Allâh (in the Hereafter) is better for those who believe and do righteous good deeds, and this none shall attain except those who are As-Sabirun (the patient in following the truth)." (80)

Quran 30:60

فَٱصْبِرْ إِنَّ وَعْدَ ٱللَّهِ حَقٌّ وَلَا يَسْتَخِفَّنَّكَ ٱلَّذِينَ لَا يُوقِنُونَ

So be patient. Verily, the Promise of Allâh is true, and let not those who have no certainty of faith, discourage you from conveying Allâh's Message (which you are obliged to convey). (60)

Quran 31:4-5

ٱلَّذِينَ يُقِيمُونَ ٱلصَّلَوٰةَ وَيُؤْتُونَ ٱلزَّكَوٰةَ وَهُم بِٱلْأَخِرَةِ هُمْ يُوقِنُونَ (٤) أُوْلَٰٓئِكَ عَلَىٰ هُدًى مِّن رَّبِّهِمْ وَأُوْلَٰٓئِكَ هُمُ ٱلْمُفْلِحُونَ (٥)

Those who perform As¬Salât (Prayers) and give Zakât and they have faith in the Hereafter with certainty. (4) Such are on guidance from their Lord, and such are the successful. (5)

Quran 31:17

يَـٰبُنَىَّ أَقِمِ ٱلصَّلَوٰةَ وَأْمُرْ بِٱلْمَعْرُوفِ وَٱنْهَ عَنِ ٱلْمُنكَرِ وَٱصْبِرْ عَلَىٰ مَآ أَصَابَكَ إِنَّ ذَٰلِكَ مِنْ عَزْمِ ٱلْأُمُورِ

"O my son! Aqim¬As¬Salât (perform Prayers), enjoin (on people) Al¬Ma'rûf (Islâmic Monotheism and all that is good), and forbid (people) from Al¬Munkar (i.e. disbelief in the Oneness of Allâh, polytheism of all kinds and all that is evil and bad), and bear with patience whatever befalls you. Verily, these are some of the important commandments (ordered by Allâh with no exemption). (17)

Quran 32:24

وَجَعَلْنَا مِنْهُمْ أَئِمَّةً يَهْدُونَ بِأَمْرِنَا لَمَّا صَبَرُواْ وَكَانُواْ بِـَٔايَـٰتِنَا يُوقِنُونَ

And We made from among them (Children of Israel), leaders, giving guidance under Our Command, when they were patient and used to believe with certainty in Our Ayât (proofs, evidences, verses, lessons, signs, revelations, etc.) (24)

Quran 33:33

وَقَرْنَ فِى بُيُوتِكُنَّ وَلَا تَبَرَّجْنَ تَبَرُّجَ ٱلْجَٰهِلِيَّةِ ٱلْأُولَىٰ وَأَقِمْنَ ٱلصَّلَوٰةَ وَءَاتِينَ ٱلزَّكَوٰةَ وَأَطِعْنَ ٱللَّهَ وَرَسُولَهُۥٓ إِنَّمَا يُرِيدُ ٱللَّهُ لِيُذْهِبَ عَنكُمُ ٱلرِّجْسَ أَهْلَ ٱلْبَيْتِ وَيُطَهِّرَكُمْ تَطْهِيرًا

And stay in your houses, and do not display yourselves like that of the times of ignorance, and perform As-Salât (Prayers), and give Zakât and obey Allâh and His Messenger. Allâh wishes only to remove Ar¬Rijs (evil deeds and sins) from you, O members of the family (of the Prophet), and to purify you with a thorough purification. (33)

Quran 35:18

وَلَا تَزِرُ وَازِرَةٌ وِزْرَ أُخْرَىٰ وَإِن تَدْعُ مُثْقَلَةٌ إِلَىٰ حِمْلِهَا لَا يُحْمَلْ مِنْهُ شَىْءٌ وَلَوْ كَانَ ذَا قُرْبَىٰٓ إِنَّمَا تُنذِرُ ٱلَّذِينَ يَخْشَوْنَ رَبَّهُم بِٱلْغَيْبِ وَأَقَامُوا۟ ٱلصَّلَوٰةَ وَمَن تَزَكَّىٰ فَإِنَّمَا يَتَزَكَّىٰ لِنَفْسِهِۦ وَإِلَى ٱللَّهِ ٱلْمَصِيرُ

And no bearer of burdens shall bear another's burden, and if one heavily laden calls another to (bear) his load, nothing of it will be lifted even though he be near of kin. You can warn only those who fear their Lord unseen, and perform As-Salât (Prayers). And he who purifies himself (from all kinds of sins), then he purifies only for the benefit of his ownself. And to Allâh is the (final) Return (of all). (18)

Quran 35:29

إِنَّ ٱلَّذِينَ يَتْلُونَ كِتَٰبَ ٱللَّهِ وَأَقَامُواْ ٱلصَّلَوٰةَ وَأَنفَقُواْ مِمَّا رَزَقْنَٰهُمْ سِرًّا وَعَلَانِيَةً يَرْجُونَ تِجَٰرَةً لَّن تَبُورَ

Verily, those who recite the Book of Allâh (this Qur'ân), and perform As¬Salât (Prayers), and spend (in charity) out of what We have provided for them, secretly and openly, they hope for a (sure) trade¬gain that will never perish. (29)

Quran 37:102

فَلَمَّا بَلَغَ مَعَهُ ٱلسَّعْىَ قَالَ يَٰبُنَىَّ إِنِّىٓ أَرَىٰ فِى ٱلْمَنَامِ أَنِّىٓ أَذْبَحُكَ فَٱنظُرْ مَاذَا تَرَىٰ قَالَ يَٰٓأَبَتِ ٱفْعَلْ مَا تُؤْمَرُ سَتَجِدُنِىٓ إِن شَآءَ ٱللَّهُ مِنَ ٱلصَّٰبِرِينَ

And, when he (his son) was old enough to walk with him, he said: "O my son! I have seen in a dream that I am slaughtering you (offer you in sacrifice to Allâh), so look what you think!" He said: "O my father! Do that which you are commanded, Inshâ' Allâh (if Allâh will), you shall find me of As-Sâbirun (the patient)." (102)

Quran 38:17

اَصْبِرْ عَلَىٰ مَا يَقُولُونَ وَاذْكُرْ عَبْدَنَا دَاوُۥدَ ذَا الْأَيْدِ إِنَّهُۥ أَوَّابٌ

Be patient of what they say, and remember Our slave Dâwûd (David), endued with power. Verily, he was ever oft-returning in all matters and in repentance (toward Allâh). (17)

Quran 38:44

وَخُذْ بِيَدِكَ ضِغْثًا فَاضْرِب بِّهِۦ وَلَا تَحْنَثْ إِنَّا وَجَدْنَٰهُ صَابِرًا نِّعْمَ الْعَبْدُ إِنَّهُۥ أَوَّابٌ

"And take in your hand a bundle of thin grass and strike therewith, and break not your oath. Truly! We found him patient. How excellent (a) slave! Verily, he was ever oft-returning in repentance (to Us)! (44)

Quran 40:55

فَاصْبِرْ إِنَّ وَعْدَ اللَّهِ حَقٌّ وَاسْتَغْفِرْ لِذَنبِكَ وَسَبِّحْ بِحَمْدِ رَبِّكَ بِالْعَشِيِّ وَالْإِبْكَٰرِ

So be patient. Verily, the Promise of Allâh is true, and ask forgiveness for your fault, and glorify the praises of your Lord in the Ashi (i.e. the time period after the midnoon till sunset) and in the Ibkâr (i.e. the time period from early morning or sunrise till before midnoon). (55)

Quran 42:38

وَٱلَّذِينَ ٱسْتَجَابُوا۟ لِرَبِّهِمْ وَأَقَامُوا۟ ٱلصَّلَوٰةَ وَأَمْرُهُمْ شُورَىٰ بَيْنَهُمْ وَمِمَّا رَزَقْنَٰهُمْ يُنفِقُونَ

And those who answer the Call of their Lord [i.e. to believe that He is the only One Lord (Allâh), and to worship none but Him Alone], and perform As-Salât (Prayers), and who (conduct) their affairs by mutual consultation, and who spend of what We have bestowed on them; (38)

Quran 47:31

وَلَنَبْلُوَنَّكُمْ حَتَّىٰ نَعْلَمَ ٱلْمُجَٰهِدِينَ مِنكُمْ وَٱلصَّٰبِرِينَ وَنَبْلُوَا۟ أَخْبَارَكُمْ

And surely, We shall try you till We test those who strive hard (for the Cause of Allâh) and As-Sabirun (the patient ones), and We shall test your facts (i.e. the one who is a liar, and the one who is truthful). (31)

Quran 52:48

وَٱصْبِرْ لِحُكْمِ رَبِّكَ فَإِنَّكَ بِأَعْيُنِنَا ۖ وَسَبِّحْ بِحَمْدِ رَبِّكَ حِينَ تَقُومُ

So wait patiently for the Decision of your Lord, for verily, you are under Our Eyes , and glorify the Praises of your Lord when you get up from sleep. (48)

Quran 54:27

إِنَّا مُرْسِلُوا ٱلنَّاقَةِ فِتْنَةً لَّهُمْ فَٱرْتَقِبْهُمْ وَٱصْطَبِرْ

Verily, We are sending the she-camel as a test for them. So watch them [O Sâlih (Saleh)], and be patient! (27)

Quran 68:48

فَٱصْبِرْ لِحُكْمِ رَبِّكَ وَلَا تَكُن كَصَاحِبِ ٱلْحُوتِ إِذْ نَادَىٰ وَهُوَ مَكْظُومٌ

So wait with patience for the Decision of your Lord, and be not like the Companion of the Fish — when he cried out (to Us) while he was in deep sorrow. (48)

Quran 70:5

فَٱصْبِرْ صَبْرًا جَمِيلًا

So be patient, with a good patience. (5)

Quran 70:19-23

۞ إِنَّ ٱلْإِنسَٰنَ خُلِقَ هَلُوعًا (١٩) إِذَا مَسَّهُ ٱلشَّرُّ جَزُوعًا (٢٠) وَإِذَا مَسَّهُ ٱلْخَيْرُ مَنُوعًا (٢١) إِلَّا ٱلْمُصَلِّينَ (٢٢) ٱلَّذِينَ هُمْ عَلَىٰ صَلَاتِهِمْ دَآئِمُونَ (٢٣)

Verily, man (disbeliever) was created very impatient; (19) Irritable (discontented) when evil touches him; (20) And niggardly when good touches him;- (21) Except those who are devoted to Salât (prayers). (22) Those who remain constant in their Salât (prayers); (23)

Quran 70:34

وَالَّذِينَ هُمْ عَلَىٰ صَلَاتِهِمْ يُحَافِظُونَ

And those who guard their Salât (prayers) well (34)

Quran 73:20

إِنَّ رَبَّكَ يَعْلَمُ أَنَّكَ تَقُومُ أَدْنَىٰ مِن ثُلُثَيِ ٱلَّيْلِ وَنِصْفَهُ وَثُلُثَهُ وَطَآئِفَةٌ مِّنَ ٱلَّذِينَ مَعَكَ وَٱللَّهُ يُقَدِّرُ ٱلَّيْلَ وَٱلنَّهَارَ عَلِمَ أَن لَّن تُحْصُوهُ فَتَابَ عَلَيْكُمْ فَٱقْرَءُوا مَا تَيَسَّرَ مِنَ ٱلْقُرْءَانِ عَلِمَ أَن سَيَكُونُ مِنكُم مَّرْضَىٰ وَءَاخَرُونَ يَضْرِبُونَ فِى ٱلْأَرْضِ يَبْتَغُونَ مِن فَضْلِ ٱللَّهِ وَءَاخَرُونَ يُقَٰتِلُونَ فِى سَبِيلِ ٱللَّهِ فَٱقْرَءُوا مَا تَيَسَّرَ مِنْهُ وَأَقِيمُوا ٱلصَّلَوٰةَ وَءَاتُوا ٱلزَّكَوٰةَ وَأَقْرِضُوا ٱللَّهَ قَرْضًا حَسَنًا وَمَا تُقَدِّمُوا لِأَنفُسِكُم مِّنْ خَيْرٍ تَجِدُوهُ عِندَ ٱللَّهِ هُوَ خَيْرًا وَأَعْظَمَ أَجْرًا وَٱسْتَغْفِرُوا ٱللَّهَ إِنَّ ٱللَّهَ غَفُورٌ رَّحِيمٌ

Verily, your Lord knows that you do stand (to pray at (also night) a little less than two-thirds of the night, or half the night, or a third of the night, and a party of those with you, And Allâh measures the night and the day. He knows that you are unable to pray the whole night, so He has turned to you (in mercy). So, recite you of the Qur'ân as much as may be easy for you. He knows that there will be some among you sick, others travelling through the land, seeking of Allâh's Bounty; yet others fighting in Allâh's Cause. So recite as much of the

Qur'ân as may be easy (for you), and perform As-Salât (Prayers) and give Zakât, and lend to Allâh a goodly loan, And whatever good you send before you for yourselves, (i.e. Nawâfil non-obligatory acts of worship: prayers, charity, fasting, Hajj and 'Umrah), you will certainly find it with Allâh, better and greater in reward. And seek Forgiveness of Allâh. Verily, Allâh is Oft-Forgiving, Most-Merciful (20)

Quran 74:7

وَلِرَبِّكَ فَٱصْبِرْ

And be patient for the sake of your Lord! (7)

Quran 74:40-43

فِى جَنَّٰتٍ يَتَسَآءَلُونَ (٤٠) عَنِ ٱلْمُجْرِمِينَ (٤١) مَا سَلَكَكُمْ فِى سَقَرَ (٤٢) قَالُواْ لَمْ نَكُ مِنَ ٱلْمُصَلِّينَ (٤٣)

In Gardens (Paradise) they will ask one another, (40) About Al-Mujrimûn (polytheists, criminals, disbelievers), (they will say to them): (41) "What has caused you to enter Hell?" (42) They will say: "We were not of those who used to offer the Salât (prayers) (43)

Quran 76:24

فَٱصْبِرْ لِحُكْمِ رَبِّكَ وَلَا تُطِعْ مِنْهُمْ ءَاثِمًا أَوْ كَفُورًا

*Therefore be patient with constancy to the Command of
your Lord (Allâh, by doing your duty to Him and by
conveying His Message to mankind), and obey neither a
sinner nor a disbeliever among them. (24)*

Quran 87:15

وَذَكَرَ ٱسْمَ رَبِّهِ فَصَلَّىٰ

*And remembers (glorifies) the Name of his Lord
(worships none but Allâh), and prays (five compulsory
prayers and Nawâfil — additional prayers). (15)*

Quran 96:10

عَبْدًا إِذَا صَلَّىٰٓ

A slave when he prays (10)

Quran 98:5

وَمَآ أُمِرُوٓاْ إِلَّا لِيَعْبُدُواْ ٱللَّهَ مُخْلِصِينَ لَهُ ٱلدِّينَ حُنَفَآءَ
وَيُقِيمُواْ ٱلصَّلَوٰةَ وَيُؤْتُواْ ٱلزَّكَوٰةَ وَذَٰلِكَ دِينُ ٱلْقَيِّمَةِ

*And they were commanded not, but that they should
worship Allâh, and worship none but Him Alone
(abstaining from ascribing partners to Him), and
perform As-Salât (Prayers) and give Zakât: and that is
the right religion. (5)*

Quran 103:1-3

وَٱلْعَصْرِ ﴿١﴾ إِنَّ ٱلْإِنسَـٰنَ لَفِى خُسْرٍ ﴿٢﴾ إِلَّا ٱلَّذِينَ ءَامَنُوا۟ وَعَمِلُوا۟ ٱلصَّـٰلِحَـٰتِ وَتَوَاصَوْا۟ بِٱلْحَقِّ وَتَوَاصَوْا۟ بِٱلصَّبْرِ ﴿٣﴾

By Al-'Asr (the time). (1) Verily, man is in loss, (2) Except those who believe (in Islâmic Monotheism) and do righteous good deeds, and recommend one another to the truth (i.e. order one another to perform all kinds of good deeds (Al-Ma'ruf) which Allâh has ordained, and abstain from all kinds of sins and evil deeds (Al-Munkar) which Allâh has forbidden), and recommend one another to patience (for the sufferings, harms, and injuries which one may encounter in Allâh's Cause during preaching His religion of Islâmic Monotheism or Jihâd). (3)

Quran 107:4-6

فَوَيْلٌ لِّلْمُصَلِّينَ ﴿٤﴾ ٱلَّذِينَ هُمْ عَن صَلَاتِهِمْ سَاهُونَ ﴿٥﴾ ٱلَّذِينَ هُمْ يُرَاءُونَ ﴿٦﴾

So woe unto those performers of Salât (prayers) (hypocrites), (4) Those who delay their Salât (prayer from their stated fixed times), (5) Those who do good deeds only to be seen (6)

Quran 108:2

فَصَلِّ لِرَبِّكَ وَٱنْحَرْ

Therefore turn in prayer to your Lord and sacrifice (to Him only) (2)

Virtuous Hadith about Patience and/or Prayer

Narrated Thabit Al-Bunani:

Anas bin Malik said to a woman of his family, "Do you know such-and-such a woman?" She replied, "Yes." He said, "The Prophet (ﷺ) passed by her while she was weeping over a grave, and he said to her, 'Be afraid of Allah and be patient.' The woman said (to the Prophet). 'Go away from me, for you do not know my calamity.'" Anas added, "The Prophet (ﷺ) left her and proceeded. A man passed by her and asked her, 'What has Allah's Messenger (ﷺ) said to you?' She replied, 'I did not recognize him.' The man said, 'He was Allah's Messenger (ﷺ).'" Anas added, "So that woman came to the gate of the Prophet (ﷺ) and she did not find a gate-keeper there, and she said, 'O Allah's Messenger (ﷺ)! By Allah. I did not recognize you!' The Prophet said, 'No doubt, patience is at the first stroke of a calamity.'"

Source: Sahih al-Bukhari 7154

It was narrated that Thabit said:

"I heard Anas say: 'The Messenger of Allah said: True patience is that which comes at the first blow.'"

Source: Sunan an-Nasa'i 1869 Grade: Sahih

It was narrated from Anas bin Malik that the Messenger of Allah (ﷺ) said:

"Patience should come with the first shock."

Source: Sunan Ibn Majah 1596 Grade: Hasan

Narrated Ibn `Abbas:

When the Verse:--'*If there are twenty steadfast amongst you (Muslims), they will overcome two hundred (non-Muslims).*' was revealed, it became hard on the Muslims when it became compulsory that one Muslim ought not to flee (in war) before ten (non-Muslims). So (Allah) lightened the order by revealing: '*(But) now Allah has lightened your (task) for He knows that there is weakness in you. So if there are of you one-hundred steadfast, they will overcome (two-hundred (non-Muslims).*' (8.66) So when Allah reduced the number of enemies which Muslims should withstand, their patience and perseverance against the enemy decreased as much as their task was lightened for them.

Source: Sahih al-Bukhari 4653

A man from Banu Sulaim narrated:

"The Messenger of Allah (ﷺ) counted them out in my hand" - or - "in his hand: 'At-Tasbīḥ is half of the Scale, and "All praise is due to Allah (Al-Ḥamdulillāh)" fills it, and At-Takbīr (Allāhu Akbar) fills what is between the sky and the earth, and fasting is half of patience, and purification is half of faith."

Source: Jami` at-Tirmidhi 3519 Grade: Hasan

It was narrated from Abu Hurairah that the Messenger of Allah (ﷺ) said:

"For everything there is Zakat and the Zakat of the body is fasting." (A narrator in one of the chains) Muhriz added in his narration: "And the Messenger of Allah (ﷺ) said: 'Fasting is half of patience.'"

Source: Sunan Ibn Majah 1745 Grade: Daif

Abu Sa'id and Abu Hurairah reported that the Prophet (ﷺ) said:

"Never a believer is stricken with a discomfort, an illness, an anxiety, a grief or mental worry or even the pricking of a thorn but Allah will expiate his sins on account of his patience".

Source: Riyad as-Salihin 37 Grade: Sahih

Abu Hurairah reported:

The Messenger of Allah (ﷺ) said, "Do not wish for an encounter with the enemy. Pray to Allah to grant you safety; (but) when you encounter them, show patience."

Source: Riyad as-Salihin 1351 Grade: Sahih

It was narrated from Ibn 'Umar that the Messenger of Allah (ﷺ) said:

"The believer who mixes with people and bears their annoyance with patience will have a greater reward than the believer who does not mix with people and does not put up with their annoyance."

Source: Sunan Ibn Majah 4032 Grade: Sahih

Ibn 'Abbas reported God's Messenger as saying: "If anyone sees in his commander what he dislikes he should show patience, for no one separates a span's distance from the community and dies without dying like those of pre-Islamic times."

Source: Mishkat al-Masabih 3668 Grade: Sahih

Abdullah bin Abu Aufa (May Allah be pleased with him) reported:

The Messenger of Allah (ﷺ) at one time when he confronted the enemy, and was waiting for the sun to set, stood up and said, "O people! Do not long for encountering the enemy and supplicate to Allah to grant you security. But when you face the enemy, show patience and steadfastness; and keep it in mind that Jannah lies under the shade of the swords." Then he invoked Allah, saying, "O Allah, Revealer of the Book, Disperser of the clouds, Defeater of the Confederates, put our enemy to rout and help us in over-powering them".

Source: Riyad as-Salihin 53 Grade: Sahih

Narrated Abu Sa`id:

Some people from the Ansar asked Allah's Messenger (ﷺ) (to give them something) and he gave to everyone of them, who asked him, until all that he had was finished. When everything was finished and he had spent all that was in his hand, he said to them, "'(Know) that if I have any wealth, I will not withhold it from you (to keep for somebody else); And (know) that he who refrains from begging others (or doing prohibited deeds), Allah will make him contented and not in need of others; and he who remains patient, Allah will bestow patience upon him, and he who is satisfied with what he has, Allah will make him self-sufficient. And there is no gift better and vast (you may be given) than patience."

Source: Sahih al-Bukhari 6470

It was narrated that Abu Hurairah said:

"A man came to the Prophet (ﷺ) while he was delivering a Khutbah from the Minbar, and he said: 'If I fight in the cause of Allah with patience and seeking reward, facing the enemy and not running away, do you think that Allah will forgive my sins?' He said: 'Yes.' Then he fell silent for a while. Then he said: 'Where is the one who was asking just now?' The man said: 'Here I am.' He said: 'What did you say?' He said: 'What did you say?' He said: 'I said: I said: If I fight in the cause of Allah with patience and seeking reward, facing the enemy and not running away, do you think that Allah will forgive my sins?' He said: 'Yes, except for debt. Jibril told me that just now.'"

Source: Sunan an-Nasa'i 3155 Grade: Sahih

Abu Musa reported that Allah's Messenger (ﷺ) said:

There is none to show more patience at listening to the most irksome things than Allah, the Exalted and Glorious. 'Partnership is associated to Him (polytheism), and (fatherhood) of a child is attributed to Him, but in spite of this He protects them (people) and provides them sustenance.' This hadith has been transmitted on the authority of Abu Musa with a slight variation of wording.

Source: Sahih Muslim 2804a, b

Narrated Um Ruman:

Who was `Aisha's mother: While I was with `Aisha, `Aisha got fever, whereupon the Prophet (ﷺ) said, "Probably her fever is caused by the story related by the people (about her)." I said, "Yes." Then `Aisha sat up and said, "My example and your example is similar to that of Jacob and his sons:--'Nay, but your minds have made up a tale. So (for me) patience is most fitting. It is Allah (alone) Whose help can be sought against that which you assert.' (12.18)

Source: Sahih al-Bukhari 4691

Narrated `Aisha:

I asked Allah's Messenger (ﷺ) about the plague. He said, "That was a means of torture which Allah used to send upon whom-so-ever He wished, but He made it a source of mercy for the believers, for anyone who is residing in a town in which this disease is present, and remains there and does not leave that town, but has patience and hopes for Allah's reward, and knows that nothing will befall him except what Allah has written for him, then he will get such reward as that of a martyr."

Source: Sahih al-Bukhari 6619

Abu Malik Al-Ash`ari narrated that the Messenger of Allah said:

"Al-Wudu is half of faith, and All praise is due to Allah (Al-Ḥamdulillāh) fills the Scale, and Glory is to Allah and all praise is to Allah (Subḥān Allāh wal-Ḥamdulillāh)' fill" - or - "fills what is between the heavens and the earth, and Salat is light and charity is an evidence, and patience is an illumination, and the Quran is a proof for you or against you. And all people shall come to the morning selling their souls, either setting it free or destroying it."

Source: Jami` at-Tirmidhi 3517 Grade: Sahih

Abu Hurairah reported:

The Messenger of Allah (ﷺ) said: "Allah, the Exalted, says: 'I have no reward except Jannah for a believing slave of Mine who shows patience and anticipates My reward when I take away his favorite one from the inhabitants of the world.'"

Source: Riyad as-Salihin 923 Grade: Sahih

It was narrated that Abu Umayyah Sha'bani said:

"I came to Abu Tha'labah Al-Khushani and said: 'How do you understand this Verse?' He said: 'Which verse?' I said: *"O you who believe! Take care of your own selves. If you follow the (right) guidance, no hurt can come to you from those who are in error."*? [5:105] He said: 'You have asked one who knows about it. I asked the Messenger of Allah (ﷺ) about it and he said: "Enjoin good upon one another and forbid one another to do evil, but if you see overwhelming stinginess, desires being followed, this world being preferred (to the Hereafter), every person with an opinion feeling proud of it, and you realize that you have no power to deal with it, then you have to mind your own business and leave the common folk to their own devices. After you will come days of patience, during which patience will be like grasping a burning ember, and one who does good deeds will have a reward like that of fifty men doing the same deed."

Source: Sunan Ibn Majah 4014 Grade: Hasan

Abu Hurairah said :

A man came to the prophet complaining against his neighbor. He said: go and have patience. He again came to him twice or thrice. He then said : Go and throw your property in the way. So he threw his property in the way and the people began to ask him and he would tell them about him. The people then began to curse him; may Allah do with him so and so! Then his neighbor came to him and said: Return, you will not see from me anything which you dislike.

Source: Sunan Abi Dawud 5153 Grade: Hasan Sahih

Mu`adh bin Jabal narrated that the Prophet (ﷺ) heard a man supplicating, saying:

"O Allah! Verily, I ask You for the bounty's completion (Allāhumma, innī as'aluka tamāman-ni`mah)." So he (ﷺ) said: "What thing is the bounty's completion?" He said: "A supplication that I made, that I hope for good by it." He (ﷺ) said: "Indeed, part of the bounty's completion is the entrance into Paradise, and salvation from the Fire." And he (ﷺ) heard a man while he was saying: "O Possessor of Majesty and Honor (Yā Dhal-Jalāli wal-Ikrām)" So he (ﷺ) said: "You have been responded to, so ask." And the Prophet (ﷺ) heard a man while he was saying: "O Allah, indeed, I ask You for patience (Allāhumma, innī as'alukas-sabr)" He (ﷺ) said: "You have asked Allah for trial, so ask him for Al-`Āfiyah(safety from afflictions).

Source: Jami` at-Tirmidhi 3527 Grade: Hasan

Amr bin sa'eed bin Abi Husain told us that:

'Amr bin Shu'aib wrote to 'Abdullah bin 'Abdur-Rahman bin Abi Husain to offer condolences for a son of his who had died. In his letter he mentioned that he had heard his father narrate, that his grandfather, 'Abdullah bin 'Amr bin Al-As said: "The Messenger of Allah said: 'Allah does not approve for His believing slave, if He takes away his loved one from among the people of the Earth, and he bears that with patience and seeks reward, and says that which he is commanded any reward less than Paradise.'"

Source: Sunan an-Nasa'i 1871 Grade: Sahih

Narrated Abu Umayah Ash-Sha'bani:

"I went to Abu Tha'balah Al-Khushani and said to him: 'How do you deal with this Ayah?' He said: 'Which Ayah?' I said: 'Allah's saying: *Take care of yourselves! If you follow the guidance no harm shall come to you* (5:105).' He said: 'Well, by Allah! I asked one well-informed about it, I asked the Messenger of Allah (ﷺ) about it. [So] he said: "Rather, comply with (and order) the good, and stay away from (and prohibit) the evil, until you see avarice obeyed, desires followed, and the world preferred, and everyone is amazed with his view. Then you should be worried about yourself in particular, and worry of the common folk. Ahead of you are the days in which patience is like holding onto an ember, for the doer (of righteous deeds) during them is the like of the reward of fifty of those who do the like of what you do." 'Abdullah bin Al-Mubarak said: "It was added for me, by other than 'Utbah, that it was said: 'O Messenger of Allah! The reward of fifty men among us, or them?' He said: 'No! Rather the reward of fifty men among you.'"

Source: Jami` at-Tirmidhi 3058 Grade: Sahih

Abdullah b. Zaid reported that when the Messenger of Allah (ﷺ) conquered Hunain he distributed the booty, and he bestowed upon those whose hearts it was intended to win. It was conveyed to him (the Prophet) that the Ansar cherished a desire that they should be given (that very portion) which the people (of Quraish) had got. Upon this the Messenger of Allah (ﷺ) stood up and, after having praised Allah and lauded Him, addressed them thus:

O people of Ansar, did I not find you erring and Allah guided you aright through me, and (in the state of) being destitute and Allah made you free from want through me, and in a state of disunity and Allah united you through me, and they (the Ansar) said: Allah and His Messenger are most benevolent. He (again) said: Why do you not answer me? They said: Allah and His Messenger are the most benevolent. He said, If you wish you should say so and so, and the event (should take) such and such course (and in this connection he made a mention) of so many things. 'Amr is under the impression that he has not been able to remember them. He (the Prophet) further said: Don't you feel happy (over this state of affairs) that the people should go away with goats and camels, and you go to your places along with the Messenger of Allah? The Ansar are inner garments (more close to me) and (other) people are outer garments. Had there not been migration, I would have been a man from among the Ansar. If the people were to tread a valley or a narrow path, I would tread the valley (chosen) by the Ansar or narrow path (trodden) by them. And you would soon find after me preferences (over you in getting material benefits). So you should show patience till you meet me at the Haud (Kauthar).

Source: Sahih Muslim 1061

It was narrated from Jabir that the Messenger of Allah (ﷺ) said:

"One prayer in my mosque is better than one thousand prayers elsewhere, except the Sacred Mosque, and one prayer in the Sacred Mosque is better than one hundred thousand prayers elsewhere."

Source: Sunan Ibn Majah 1406 Grade: Sahih

It was narrated that Anas bin Malik said:

"The Messenger of Allah (ﷺ) said: 'A man's prayer in his house is equal (in reward) to one prayer; his prayer in the mosque of the tribes is equal to twenty-five prayers; his prayer in the mosque in which Friday prayer is offered is equal to five-hundred prayers; his prayer in Aqsa Mosque is equal to fifty thousand prayers; his prayer in my mosque is equal to fifty thousand prayers; and his prayer in the Sacred Mosque is equal to one hundred thousand prayers."

Source: Sunan Ibn Majah 1413 Grade: Daif

It was narrated from that the Prophet (ﷺ) said:

"Prayer in congregation is twenty-five levels better than a prayer offered on one's own."

Source: Sunan an-Nasa'i 839 Grade: Sahih

Narrated Abu Umamah:

The Prophet (ﷺ) said: Prayer followed by a prayer with no idle talk between the two is recorded in Illiyyun.

Source: Sunan Abi Dawud 1288 Grade: Hasan

Abd Allah bin Buraidah said :

'Imran b. Hussain asked the prophet (ﷺ) about the prayer a man offers in sitting condition. He replied: his prayer in standing condition is better than his prayer in sitting condition, and his prayer in sitting condition is half the prayer he offers in standing condition, and his prayer in lying condition is half the prayer he offers in sitting condition.

Source: Sunan Abi Dawud 951 Grade: Sahih

Abu Huraira reported that the Messenger of Allah (ﷺ) said:

The five (daily) prayers and one Friday prayer to (the next) Friday prayer are expiations (for the sins committed in the intervals) between them.

Source: Sahih Muslim 233b

Narrated Abu Huraira:

Allah's Messenger (ﷺ) said, "If the Imam leads the prayer correctly then he and you will receive the rewards but if he makes a mistake (in the prayer) then you will receive the reward for the prayer and the sin will be his."

Source: Sahih al-Bukhari 694

Mujahid said:

"Ibn Abbas was asked about a man who fasted during the day and stood (in prayers) during the night, but he did not attend the Friday prayer nor congregational prayer. He replied: 'He is in the Fire.'"

Source: Jami` at-Tirmidhi 218 Grade: Daif

Narrated Abu Hurairah:

The Messenger of Allah (ﷺ) as saying: The most excellent fast after Ramadan is Allah's month al-Muharram, and the most excellent prayer after the prescribed prayer is the prayer during night.

Source: Sunan Abi Dawud 2429 Grade: Sahih

Narrated Ibn `Umar:

The Prophet (ﷺ) saw expectoration in the direction of the Qibla of the mosque while he was leading the prayer, and scratched it off. After finishing the prayer, he said, "Whenever any of you is in prayer he should know that Allah is in front of him. So none should spit in front of him in the prayer."

Source: Sahih al-Bukhari 753

It was narrated that Ibn 'Umar said:

"The Messenger of Allah said: 'The prayer of a man in congregation is twenty-seven levels more virtuous than a man's prayer on his own.'"

Source: Sunan Ibn Majah 789 Grade: Sahih

Narrated Abu Huraira:

Allah's Messenger (ﷺ) said, "If the people knew what is the reward of making the call (for the prayer) and (of being in) the first row (in the prayer), and if they found no other way to get this privilege except by casting lots, they would certainly cast lots for it. If they knew the reward of the noon prayer, they would race for it, and if they knew the reward of the morning (i.e. Fajr) and `Isha prayers, they would present themselves for the prayer even if they had to crawl to reach there.

Source: Sahih al-Bukhari 2689

Abu Hurairah reported:

The Messenger of Allah (ﷺ) said, "Everyone among you will be deemed to be occupied in Salat (prayer) constantly so long as Salat (the prayer) detains him (from worldly concerns), and nothing prevents him from returning to his family but Salat."

Source: Riyad as-Salihin 1061 Grade: Sahih

Jabir reported Allah's Messenger (ﷺ) as saying:

When any one of you observes prayer in the mosque he should reserve a part of his prayer for his house, for Allah would make the prayer as a means of betterment in his house.

Source: Sahih Muslim 778

It was narrated that Thawban said:

"The Messenger of Allah said: 'Adhere to righteousness even though you will not be able to do all acts of virtue. Know that the best of your deeds is Salat (prayer) and that no one maintains his ablution except a believer.'"

Source: Sunan Ibn Majah 277 Grade: Hasan

Ibn Umar narrated that :

the Prophet said: "Whoever misses the Asr prayer, then it is as if he was robbed of his family and his property."

Source: Jami` at-Tirmidhi 175 Grade: Sahih

It was narrated that Buraidah Al-Aslami said:

"We were with the Messenger of Allah on a campaign, and he said: 'Hasten to perform prayer on a cloudy day, for whoever misses the 'Asr prayer, all his good deeds will be in vain.'"

Source: Sunan Ibn Majah 694 Grade: Sahih

It is reported on the authority of 'Abdullah that the Messenger of Allah observed:

The best of' the deeds or deed is the (observance of) prayer at its proper time and kindness to the parents.

Source: Sahih Muslim 85e

Zaid bin Thabit narrated that:

The Prophet said: "The most virtuous prayer of yours is in your homes, except for the obligatory."

Source: Jami` at-Tirmidhi 450 Grade: Sahih

Jabir narrated:

"It was said to the Prophet: 'Which Salat is most virtuous?' He said: 'That with the longest Qunut.'"

Source: Jami` at-Tirmidhi 387 Grade: Sahih

Ibn Umar narrated that :

The Prophet said: "Offer Salat in your homes and do not turn them into graves."

Source: Jami` at-Tirmidhi 451 Grade: Sahih

It was narrated that 'Abdullah bin Salam said:

"I said, when the Messenger of Allah (ﷺ) was sitting: 'We find in the Book of Allah that on Friday there is an hour when no believing slave performs prayer and asks Allah for anything at that time, but Allah will fulfill his need.'" 'Abdullah said: "The Messenger of Allah (ﷺ) pointed to me, saying: 'Or some part of an hour.' I said: 'you are right, or some part of an hour.' I said: 'What time is that?' He said: 'It is the last hours of the day.' I said: 'It is not the time of the prayer?' He said: 'Yes (it is so), when a believing slave performs prayer and then sits with nothing but the prayer keeping him, he is still in a state of prayer.'"

Source: Sunan Ibn Majah 1139 Grade: Hasan

Narrated Abu Huraira:

Allah's Messenger (ﷺ) said, "The congregational prayer of anyone amongst you is more than twenty (five or twenty seven) times in reward than his prayer in the market or in his house, for if he performs ablution completely and then goes to the mosque with the sole intention of performing the prayer, and nothing urges him to proceed to the mosque except the prayer, then, on every step which he takes towards the mosque, he will be raised one degree or one of his sins will be forgiven. The angels will keep on asking Allah's forgiveness and blessings for everyone of you so long as he keeps sitting at his praying place. The angels will say, 'O Allah, bless him! O Allah, be merciful to him!' as long as he does not do Hadath or a thing which gives trouble to the other." The Prophet (ﷺ) further said, "One is regarded in prayer so long as one is waiting for the prayer."

Source: Sahih al-Bukhari 2119

Anas bin Malik narrated:

"On the Night of Isra, fifty prayers were made obligatory upon the Prophet. Then it was decreased until it was made five. Then it was called out: 'O Muhammad! Indeed My Word does not change; these five prayers will be recorded for you as fifty.'"

Source: Jami` at-Tirmidhi 213 Grade: Sahih

It was narrated that Salman said:

"The Messenger of Allah (ﷺ) said to me: 'There is no man who purifies himself on Friday as he is commanded, then comes out of his house to the Friday prayer, and listens attentively until he finishes his prayer, but it will be an expiation for what came before it the week before."

Source: Sunan an-Nasa'i 1403 Grade: Sahih

It was narrated from 'Umar bin Khattab that:

The Prophet used to say: "Whoever performs prayer in congregation at the mosque for forty nights, never missing the first Rak'ah of the 'Isha' prayer, Allah will thereby decree for him salvation from the Fire."

Source: Sunan Ibn Majah 798 Grade: Daif

Abdullah bin Mas'ud (May Allah be pleased with him) reported:

A man kissed a woman and he came to the Prophet (ﷺ) and made a mention of that to him. It was (on this occasion) that this Ayah was revealed:

"And perform As-Salat (Iqamat-As-Salat), at the two ends of the day and in some hours of the night [i.e., the five compulsory Salat (prayers)]. Verily, the good deeds remove the evil deeds (i.e., small sins)". (11:114)

That person said, "O Messenger of Allah (ﷺ), does it concern me only?". He (Messenger of Allah (ﷺ)) said, "It concerns the whole of my Ummah".

Source: Riyad as-Salihin 434 Grade: Sahih

Narrated AbuUmamah:

The Messenger of Allah (ﷺ) said: If anyone goes out from his house after performing ablution for saying the prescribed prayer in congregation (in the mosque), his reward will be like that of one who goes for hajj pilgrimage after wearing ihram (robe worn by the hajj pilgrims).

And he who goes out to say the mid-morning (duha) prayer, and takes the trouble for this purpose, will take the reward like that of a person who performs umrah. And a prayer followed by a prayer with no worldly talk during the gap between them will be recorded in Illiyyun.

Source: Sunan Abi Dawud 558 Grade: Hasan

It was narrated from Samurah bin Jundab that the Prophet (ﷺ) said:

"Whoever offers the morning prayer, he is under the protection of Allah, the Mighty and Sublime."

Source: Sunan Ibn Majah 3946 Grade: Sahih

Abu Hurairah reported:

Messenger of Allah (ﷺ) said, "Should I not direct you to something by which Allah obliterates the sins and elevates (your) ranks." They said: "Yes, O Messenger of Allah". He said, "Performing Wudu' properly, even in difficulty, frequently going to the mosque, and waiting eagerly for the next Salat (prayer) after a Salat is over; indeed, that is Ar-Ribat".

Source: Riyad as-Salihin 131 Grade: Sahih

Abu Musa reported:

The Messenger of Allah (ﷺ) said, "The person who will receive the highest reward for Salat (prayer) is the one who comes to perform it in the mosque from the farthest distance. And he who waits for Salat to perform it with the Imam (in congregation) will have a greater reward than the one who observes it alone and then goes to sleep."

Source: Riyad as-Salihin 1057 Grade: Sahih

Uthman b. 'Affan reported:

The Messenger of Allah as saying: "if anyone says the night prayer in congregation, he is like one who keeps vigil (in prayer) till midnight; and he who says both the night and dawn prayer in congregation is like one who keeps vigil (in prayer) the whole night."

Source: Sunan Abi Dawud 555 Grade: Sahih

It was narrated that Abu Hurairah said:

"The Messenger of Allah said: 'When one of you enters the mosque, he is in a state of prayer, so long as the prayer keeps him there, and the angels will send prayer upon anyone of you so long as he remains in the place where he prayed, saying: "O Allah, forgive him; O Allah, have mercy on him; O Allah, accept his repentance," so long as he does not commit Hadath nor disturb anyone.'"

Source: Sunan Ibn Majah 799 Grade: Sahih

Anas bin Malik reported:

A man came to the Prophet (ﷺ) and said, "O Messenger of Allah, I have committed a sin liable of ordained punishment. So execute punishment on me". Messenger of Allah (ﷺ) did not ask him about it, and then came the (time for) Salat (prayers). So he performed Salat with Messenger of Allah (ﷺ). When Messenger of Allah (ﷺ) finished Salat, the man stood up and said: "O Messenger of Allah! I have committed a sin. So execute the Ordinance of Allah upon me". He (ﷺ) asked, "Have you performed Salat with us?" "Yes", he replied. Messenger of Allah (ﷺ) said, "Verily, Allah has forgiven you".

Source: Riyad as-Salihin 435 Grade: Sahih

Narrated Ibn `Abbas:

I brought water to `Uthman bin `Affan to perform the ablution while he was sitting on his seat. He performed the ablution in a perfect way and said, "I saw the Prophet (ﷺ) performing the ablution in this place and he performed it in a perfect way and said, "Whoever performs the ablution as I have done this time and then proceeds to the mosque and offers a two-rak`at prayer and then sits there (waiting for the compulsory congregational prayers), then all his past sins will be forgiven." The Prophet (ﷺ) further added, "Do not be conceited" (thinking that your sins will be forgiven because of your prayer).

Source: Sahih al-Bukhari 6433

Abu Hurairah reported:

The Messenger of Allah (ﷺ) said, "There are angels who take turns in visiting you by night and by day, and they all assemble at the dawn (Fajr) and the afternoon ('Asr) prayers. Those who have spent the night with you, ascend to the heaven and their Rabb, Who knows better about them, asks: 'In what condition did you leave My slaves?' They reply: 'We left them while they were performing Salat and we went to them while they were performing Salat.'"

Source: Riyad as-Salihin 1050 Grade: Sahih

Abu Bakr reported on the authority of his father that the Messenger of Allah (ﷺ) said:

He who observed two prayers at two cool (hours) would enter Paradise.

Source: Sahih Muslim 635a

Narrated Abu Huraira:

Allah's Messenger (ﷺ) said: "Whoever establishes prayers during the nights of Ramadan faithfully out of sincere faith and hoping to attain Allah's rewards (not for showing off), all his past sins will be forgiven."

Source: Sahih al-Bukhari 37

Umm Farwah - and she was one of those who gave pledge of allegiance to the Prophet - narrated:

"The Prophet was asked: 'Which deed is the best?' So he said: 'Salat in the beginning of its time.'"

Source: Jami` at-Tirmidhi 170 Grade: Sahih

It was narrated that Umm Habibah said:

"The Messenger of Allah (ﷺ) said: 'Whoever prays twelve rak'ahs in a day apart from the obligatory prayers, Allah will build for him, or there will be built for him, a house in Paradise.'"

Source: Sunan an-Nasa'i 1808

Rafi' bin Khadij reported the Messenger of Allah (ﷺ) as saying:

Offer Fajr prayer at dawn, for it is most productive of rewards to you or most productive of reward.

Source: Sunan Abi Dawud 424 Grade: Hasan Sahih

It was narrated that Abu Dharr said:

"The Messenger of Allah (ﷺ) said: 'When anyone of you gets up to perform prayer, then indeed mercy is facing him, so he should not smooth the pebbles.'"

Source: Sunan Ibn Majah 1027 Grade: Hasan

Abu Hurairahu reported:

I heard the Messenger of Allah (ﷺ) saying, "Say, if there were a river at the door of one of you in which he takes a bath five times a day, would any soiling remain on him?" They replied, "No soiling would left on him." He (ﷺ) said, " That is the five (obligatory) Salat (prayers). Allah obliterates all sins as a result of performing them."

Source: Riyad as-Salihin 1042 Grade: Sahih

Anas bin Malik narrated that :

Allah's Messenger said: "Whoever performs Salat for Allah for forty days in congregation, catching the first Takbir, two absolutions are written for him: absolution from the Fire, and absolution from the Fire, and absolution from hypocrisy."

Source: Jami` at-Tirmidhi 241 Grade: Daif

Thauban said:

I heard Messenger of Allah (ﷺ) saying, "Perform Salah more often. For every prostration that you perform before Allah will raise your position one degree and will remit one of your sins".

Source: Riyad as-Salihin 107 Grade: Sahih

It was narrated that 'Abdullah bin Mas'ud said:

"I asked the Messenger of Allah (ﷺ) which action is most beloved to Allah? He said: 'Establishing prayer on time, honoring one's parents and Jihad in the cause of Allah.'"

Source: Sunan an-Nasa'i 611 Grade: Sahih

It was narrated from Mus'ab bin Sa'd, from his father, that he thought he was better than other Companions of the Prophet (ﷺ). The Prophet of Allah (ﷺ) said:

"Rather, Allah support this Ummah because of their supplication, their Salah, and their sincerity."

Source: Sunan an-Nasa'i 3178 Grade: Sahih

It was narrated that 'Abdullah bin 'Amr said:

"The Messenger of Allah said: 'Adhere to righteousness even though you will not be able to do all acts of virtue. Know that among the best of your deeds is prayer and that no one maintains his ablution except a believer.'"

Source: Sunan Ibn Majah 278 Grade: Hasan

Narrated Abu Huraira:

The Prophet (ﷺ) said, "Angels keep on descending from and ascending to the Heaven in turn, some at night and some by daytime, and all of them assemble together at the time of the Fajr and `Asr prayers. Then those who have stayed with you over-night, ascent unto Allah Who asks them, and He knows the answer better than they, "How have you left My slaves?" They reply, "We have left them praying as we found them praying." If anyone of you says "Amin" (during the Prayer at the end of the recitation of Surat-al-Faitiha), and the angels in Heaven say the same, and the two sayings coincide, all his past sins will be forgiven."

Source: Sahih al-Bukhari 3223

It was narrated from Abu Hurairah that the Messenger of Allah (ﷺ) said:

"When Friday comes, angels stand at every door of the mosque and record the names of the people who come, in order of arrival. When the Imam comes out, they close their records and listen to the sermon. The first one who comes to the prayer is like one who sacrifices a camel; the one who comes after him is like one who sacrifices a cow; the one who comes after him is like one who sacrifices a ram," (and so on) until he made mention of a hen and an egg. Sahl added in his Hadith: "And whoever comes after that comes only to do his duty with regard to the prayer."

Source: Sunan Ibn Majah 1092 Grade: Sahih

It was narrated that Humran bin Aban said:

We were with `Uthman bin `Affan, he called for water and did wudoo'. When he had finished his wudoo`, he smiled and said: Do you know why I smiled? He said: The Messenger of Allah (ﷺ) did wudoo` as I just did wudoo`, then he smiled and said: "Do you know why I smiled?` we said: Allah and His Messenger know best. He said: "If a person does wudoo and completes his wudoo', then he starts to pray and completes his prayer, he will come out of his prayer free of sin as he came out of his mother`s womb."

Source: Musnad Ahmad 430 Grade: Sahih

Narrated Salman-Al-Farsi:

The Prophet said, "Whoever takes a bath on Friday, purifies himself as much as he can, then uses his (hair) oil or perfumes himself with the scent of his house, then proceeds (for the Jumua prayer) and does not separate two persons sitting together (in the mosque), then prays as much as (Allah has) written for him and then remains silent while the Imam is delivering the Khutba, his sins in-between the present and the last Friday would be forgiven."

Source: Sahih al-Bukhari 883

Narrated Abu Huraira:

The Prophet (ﷺ) said, "Charity is obligatory everyday on every joint of a human being. If one helps a person in matters concerning his riding animal by helping him to ride it or by lifting his luggage on to it, all this will be regarded charity. A good word, and every step one takes to offer the compulsory Congregational prayer, is regarded as charity; and guiding somebody on the road is regarded as charity."

Source: Sahih al-Bukhari 2891

It was narrated that 'Ubadah bin Samit said:

"I heard the Messenger of Allah (ﷺ) say: 'Five prayers that Allah has enjoined upon His slaves, so whoever does them, and does not omit anything out of negligence, on the Day of Resurrection Allah will make a covenant with him that He will admit him to Paradise. But whoever does them but omits something from them out of negligence, will not have such a covenant with Allah; if He wills He will punish him, and if He wills, He will forgive him.'"

Source: Sunan Ibn Majah 1401 Grade: Hasan

It was narrated from Abu Bakr Siddiq that the Messenger of Allah (ﷺ) said:

"Whoever offers the morning prayer, he is under the protection of Allah, so do not betray Allah by betraying those who are under His protection. Whoever kills him, Allah will seek him out until He throws him on his face into Hell."

Source: Sunan Ibn Majah 3945 Grade: Sahih

It was narrated from Abu Umamah that the Messenger of Allah (ﷺ) said:

"The one who most deserved to be envied, in my view, is the one who has the least burden, who prays a great deal and finds joy in prayer, and who is unknown among people and is not paid any heed. His provision will be sufficient, he will be content with it, his death will come quickly, his estate will be small and his mourners will be few."

Source: Sunan Ibn Majah 4117 Grade: Daif

Narrated Abdullah ibn Amr ibn al-'As:

The Prophet (ﷺ) said: Three types of people attend Friday prayer; One is present in a frivolous way and that is all he gets from it; another comes with a supplication, Allah may grant or refuse his request as He wishes; another is present silently and quietly with-out stepping over a Muslim or annoying anyone, and that is an atonement for his sins till the next Friday and three days more, the reason being that Allah, the Exalted, says: "He who does a good deed will have ten times as much" (vi.160).

Source: Sunan Abi Dawud 1113 Grade: Hasan

Uqbah b. 'Amir said:

We served ourselves in the company of Messenger of Allah (ﷺ). We tended our camels by turn. One day I had my turn to tend the camels, and I drove them in the afternoon. I found the Messenger of Allah (ﷺ) addressing the people. I heard him say: Anyone amongst you who performs ablution, and does it well, then he stands and offers two rak'ahs of prayer, concentrating on it with his heart and body, Paradise will be his lot by all means. I said: Ha-ha! How fine it is! A man in front of me said: The action (mentioned by the Prophet) earlier, O 'Uqbah, is finer that this one. I looked at him and found him to be 'Umar b. al-Khattab. I asked him: What is that, O Abu Hafs? He replied: He (the Prophet) had said before you came: If any one of you performs ablution, and does it well, and when he finishes the ablution, he utters the words : I bear witness that there is no deity except Allah, He has no associate, and I bear witness that Muhammad is His Servant and His Messenger, all the eight doors of Paradise will be opened for him; he may enter (through) any of them.

Mu'awiyah said: Rabi'ah b. Yazid narrated this tradition to me from Abu Idris and the authority of 'Uqbah b.'Amir.

Source: Sunan Abi Dawud 169 Grade: Sahih

It was narrated that Abu Hurairah said, 'I heard the Messenger of Allah(ﷺ) say':

"Allah said: 'I have divided the prayer between Myself and My slave into two halves, and My slave shall have what he has asked for.'When the slave says: 'Al-hamdulillah i rabbil Alameen (All the praise is to Allah, the Lord of all that exists),' Allah says:'My slave has praised Me, and My slave shall have what he has asked for.' And when he says: 'Ar-Rahmanir-Rahim (The Mos Gracious, the Most Merciful),' Allah says: 'My slave has extolled Me, and My slave shall have what he has asked for.' And when he says: 'Maliki yawmiddin [The Only Owner (and he Ruling Judge] if the Day of Recompense],' Allahs says: 'My slave has Glorified Me. This is for Me, and this Verse is between me and My slave in two halves.' And when he says: ' Iyyaka na'budu wa iyyaka nastain [You (Alone) we worship, and You (Alone) we ask for help],' He says: 'This is between Me an My slave, and My slave shall have what he has asked for.' And the end of the Surah is for My slave.' And when he says: 'Ihdinas-siratal-mustaqeema, siratal-alldhina an'amta alayhim wa lad-dallin [Guide us to the Straight Way, the way of those on whom You have bestowed Your Grace, not(the way) of those who earned Your Anger, nor of those who went astray],' He says: 'This is for My slave, and My slave shall have what he has asked for."

Source: Sunan Ibn Majah 3784 Grade: Sahih

Narrated Jabir:

that the Prophet (ﷺ) said: "Between disbelief and faith is abandoning the Salat."

Source: Jami` at-Tirmidhi 2618 Grade: Sahih

Abdullah bin Buraidah narrated that his father said:

"The Messenger of Allah (ﷺ) said: 'The covenant that distinguishes between us and them is prayer; so whoever leaves it, he has committed Kufr.'"

Source: Sunan Ibn Majah 1079 Grade: Sahih

Narrated Abdullah ibn Amr ibn al-'As:

The Messenger of Allah (ﷺ) said: Command your children to pray when they become seven (lunar) years old, and beat them for it (prayer) when they become ten (lunar) years old; and arrange their beds (to sleep) separately.

Source: Sunan Abi Dawud 495 Grade: Hasan Sahih

Jabir bin 'Abdullah, narrated that :

Allah's Messenger said: "The key to Paradise is Salat, and the key to Salat is Wudu'."

Source: Jami` at-Tirmidhi 4 Grade: Hasan

Sahl As-Sa'idi, said:

"I heard the Messenger of Allah (ﷺ) say: 'Whoever is in the Masjid waiting for the prayer, he is in a state of prayer.'"

Source: Sunan an-Nasa'i 734 Grade: Hasan

It was narrated that Abu Hurairah said:

"The Messenger of Allah said: 'When one of you performs ablution and does it well, then he comes to the mosque with no other motive but prayer and not seeking anything other than the prayer, he does not take one step but Allah raises him in status one degree thereby, and takes away one of his sins, until he enters the mosque. When he enters the mosque he is in a state of prayer so long as he is waiting for the prayer.'"

Source: Sunan Ibn Majah 774 Grade: Sahih

Ali reported that the last words of the Prophet, may Allah bless him and grant him peace, were:

"The prayer! The prayer! Fear Allah concerning your slaves!"

Source: Al-Adab Al-Mufrad 158 Grade: Sahih

Narrated Ali ibn AbuTalib: The last words which the Messenger of Allah (ﷺ) spoke were:

Prayer, prayer; fear Allah about those whom your right hands possess.

Source: Sunan Abi Dawud 5156 Grade: Sahih

It was narrated from `Ali that he said:

`The last words of the Messenger of Allah (ﷺ) were: "Prayer, prayer! And fear Allah with regard to what your right hands possess."

Source: Musnad Ahmad 585 Grade: Sahih

It was narrated from Umm Salamah that the Messenger of Allah (ﷺ) used to say, during the illness that would be his last:

"The prayer, and those whom your hands possess." And he kept on saying it until his tongue could no longer utter any words.

Source: Sunan Ibn Majah 1625 Grade: Daif

It was narrated from Tamim Dari that the Prophet (ﷺ) said:

"The first thing for which a person will be brought to account on the Day of Resurrection will be his prayer. If it is complete, then the voluntary (prayers) will also be recorded for him (as an increase). If it is not complete then Allah will say to His angels: 'Look and see whether you find any voluntary prayers for My slave, and take them to make up what is lacking from his obligatory prayers.' Then all his deeds will be reckoned in like manner."

Source: Sunan Ibn Majah 1426 Grade: Sahih

www.ingramcontent.com/pod-product-compliance
Lightning Source LLC
Chambersburg PA
CBHW061655120626
46550CB00003B/949